Sectional Maps
of Britain's Railways
as at 2002

INTRODUCTION

Until the late 1980s, one of the regular atlases published by Ian Allan Publishing was the Sectional Atlas which showed the extant railway lines in the country alongside the closed lines, thereby allowing the historian and enthusiast to identify the relationship between open and closed lines.

The last edition of the *Sectional Atlas* was published in the late 1980s and, in the decade or more since the last edition appeared, the railway industry has been transformed with the arrival of privatisation and the creation of franchises for individual parts of the network. Alongside a continuing — but less dramatic — diminution in the scale of the freight-only network, there has been the growth in second-generation LRT schemes and in preservation.

This new edition of *Sectional Atlas* has been prepared using Ian Allan Publishing Ltd's new computer database of the railway network and has been brought into a format similar to the other railway atlases published by the company over the past few years.

Every effort has been made to ensure that the atlas is as correct and as up to date as possible. One area of potential debate is the status of disused freight lines, of which a significant number exist with new lines (such as that to Wisbech) being added to this pool. Some of these lines may well end up as preservation schemes; others may well ultimately be lifted. Users will note that there have been a substantial number of changes since the last edition was prepared, in particular with the loss of the traditional Regional boundaries, but it is hoped that the presentation is clearer and more easily used.

As always, the Publishers will welcome any corrections or updates for incorporation into any future edition of the atlas.

Front cover: SouthWest Trains operated Class 159, No 159021, passing an EWS-liveried Class 66 at Eastleigh on 6 November 2001.

Back cover, top: Scotrail Class 158, No158734, seen under the canopy at Wick on 22 August 2001.

Back cover, bottom: First Great Western Class 180 Adelante unit, No 180104, alongside a Heathrow Express Class 332, No 332012, at paddington on 28 December 2001. *All illustrations by Brian Morrison*

First published 2002

ISBN 0 7110 2878 8

© Ian Allan Publishing 2002

Published by Ian Allan Publishing

an imprint of Ian Allan Publishing Ltd, Hersham, Surrey KT12 4RG.

Printed by Ian Allan Printing Ltd, Hersham, Surrey KT12 4RG.

Code: 0209/B2

KEY PAGE

—————————————————————— passenger line open

————————————————————— passenger line proposed or under construction

- - - - - - - - - - - - - - - - passenger line in tunnel

—————————————————————— freight line proposed or under construction

—————————————————————— freight

—————————————————————— other non-preserved passenger lines

· · · · · · · · · · · · · · · · other non-preserved passenger lines in tunnel

—————————————————————— preserved lines

- - - - - - - - - - - - - - - - preserved lines proposed or under construction

—————————————————————— line closed

BATTLE   open passenger station

THAMESPORT   freight facility

HAWKHURST   closed station

1 2 3 Seven 4 5

A
B
C
D
E
F
G

Plymouth inset:

PLYMOUTH

KEYHAM
DEVONPORT
DEVONPORT DOCKYARD
DEVONPORT (DOCKS)
Devonport Jc.
West Jc.
PLYMOUTH NORTH RD. Jc.
South Jc.
Lipson Jc.
Laira Jc.
Mount Gould Jc.
Friary Jc.
Cattewater Jc.
DEVONPORT
FRIARY
CATTEWATER
PLYMSTOCK
TURNCHAPEL

Main map:

BUDE
HALWILL JUNC. & BEAWORTHY
NEWMILL
Launceston Steam Railway
LAUNCESTON
PADSTOW
WENFORD
CHEESEWRING QUARRY
TAVISTOCK
WADEBRIDGE
CALLINGTON
GUNNISLAKE
Shillamill Tun.
Grogley Jc.
BOSCARNE JUNCTION
BODMIN GENERAL
COLESLOGGETT HALT
CALSTOCK
BERE ALSTON
Bodmin & Wenford Railway
MOORSWATER
Moorswater Jc.
BERE FERRERS
Brownqueen Tun.
BODMIN PARKWAY
LISKEARD
NEWQUAY
QUINTRELL DOWNS
St. Dennis Jc.
ROCHE
COOMBE
MENHENIOT
ST. BUDEAUX FERRY RD
Tolcarn Jc.
BUGLE
ST. KEYNE
Royal Albert Bridge
SALTASH
ST. BUDEAUX VICTORIA RD
BENNY HALT
Lappa Valley Railway
ST. COLUMB RD.
LUXULYAN
LOSTWITHIEL
CAUSELAND
KEYHAM
PLYMOUTH
DRINNICK MILL
Treverrin Tun.
SAINT GERMANS
DEVONPORT
PERRANPORTH
PARKANDILLACK
PAR
SANDPLACE
Wivelscombe Tun.
ST. AUSTELL
FOWEY
LOOE
PLYMOUTH
Polperro Tun.
Buckshead Tun.
TRURO
PORTREATH (Goods)
Penwithers Jc.
NEWHAM (Goods)
ST. IVES
Redruth Jc.
REDRUTH
PERRANWELL
CARBIS BAY
ROSKEAR
CAMBORNE
TRESAVEAN
Perran Tun.
LELANT
LELANT SALTINGS
HAYLE
ST. ERTH
PENRYN
PENMERE
PENZANCE
FALMOUTH DOCKS
TOWN
HELSTON

E
F

5 Seven 4 3 2 Eight 1

Three

A

B

C

D

E

F

G

TIVERTON
TIVERTON PARKWAY
HEMYOCK

EGGESFORD
LAPFORD
MORCHARD ROAD
COPPLESTONE

Summit
HONITON
Honiton Tun.

FENITON

AXMINSTER

Coleford Jc.
CREDITON
YEOFORD
NEWTON ST. CYRES

WHIMPLE

COLYTON

Limited Seasonal
Service

MELDON
QUARRY
OKEHAMPTON
Dartmoor Railway
Meldon Jc.
Summit

Cowley Bridge Jc.
ST
JAMES
PARK Exmouth Jc.
ST. DAVIDS
PINHOE
POLSLOE BRIDGE
ST. THOMAS
City Bosin Jc.
CENTRAL
EXETER
DIGBY & SOWTON
MARSH BARTON

COLYFORD
Seaton
Tramway
SEATON

Yes Tor

TOPSHAM

EXTON
LYMPSTONE COMMANDO
LYMPSTONE VILLAGE

SIDMOUTH

MORETON
HAMPSTEAD

STARCROSS
EXMOUTH
BUDLEIGH SALTERTON

DAWLISH WARREN

DAWLISH

PRINCETOWN

HEATHFIELD

TEIGNMOUTH

ASHBURTON
NEWTON ABBOT
Aller Jc.

Summit
Dainton Tun.
TORRE

BUCKFASTLEIGH
South Devon
Railway
STAVERTON

TORQUAY

TOTNES (LITTLEHEMPSTON)
Marley
Tun.
Ashburton Jc.
TOTNES
PAIGNTON
PAIGNTON QUEENS PARK
GOODRINGTON SANDS

Summit
IVYBRIDGE

Tavistock Jc.

CHURSTON
Greenway Tun.
BRIXHAM
Paignton &
Dartmouth
Steam Railway
KINGSWEAR

YEALMPTON

KINGSBRIDGE

1 2 Eight 3 4 Nine 5

A

ROYAL PORTBURY DOCK
AVONMOUTH
PORTISHEAD
SHIREHAMPTON
SEA MILLS
FILTON ABBEY WOOD
Westerleigh Junc.
CHIPPENHAM
CLEVEDON
BRISTOL
CLIFTON DOWN
St Annes Park Jun.
SEE INSET
St Annes Park Jun.
Brislington Tuns.
OLDLAND COMMON
BITTON
Avon Valley Railway
Thingley Jc.
CALNE
NAILSEA & BACKWELL
St Anne's Wood Tun.
KEYNSHAM
SALTFORD (proposed)
Box Tun.
YATTON
Twerton Tun.
OLDFIELD PARK
Middle Hill Tun.
MELKSHAM
WORLE
Devonshire Tun.
Bathampton Junc.
Worle Jun.
Combe Down Tun.
BATH SPA
WESTON MILTON
BRADFORD ON AVON
Bradford Jcs.
DEVIZES
WESTON SUPER MARE
BLAGDON
FRESHFORD
Uphill Junc.
AVONCLIFF
TROWBRIDGE

B

BURNHAM
CHEDDAR
RADSTOCK
Somerset and Avon Railway
WESTBURY
HIGHBRIDGE & BURNHAM
Chilcompton Tun.
MELLS ROAD
Fairwood Jc.
Heywood Road Jc.
Masbury Summit
VOBSTER
DILTON MARSH
WELLS
WHATLEY QUARRY
Clink Road Jc.
WARMINSTER
Winsor Hill Tun.
FROME
CRANMORE WEST
CRANMORE
MEREHEAD
Blatchbridge Jc.
SHEPTON MALLET
MERRYFIELD LANE
MENDIP VALE
East Somerset Railway
GLASTONBURY & STREET
Witham East Somerset Jc.
EVERCREECH (NEW)

C

BRIDGWATER
EVERCREECH JUNC.
CASTLE CARY
BRUTON
Castle Cary Junc.

D

Athelney Junc.
TISBURY
Curry Rivell Junc.
Somerton Tunnel
GILLINGHAM
TEMPLECOMBE
Buckhorn Weston Tun.
Summit
YEOVIL PEN MILL
Clifton Maybank Jc
SHERBORNE

E

YEOVIL JUNCTION
THORNFORD
CHARD
CREWKERNE
YETMINSTER
Crewkerne Tunnel
CHETNOLE
BLANDFORD
Evershot Tunnel
WEST MOORS

WIMBORNE

F

MAIDEN NEWTON
Corfe Mullen Junc.
BRANKSOME
Poundbury Tunnel
HAMWORTHY (Goods)
Hales Bay Jc.
Gasworks Jc.
BOURNEMOUTH
BRIDPORT
LYME REGIS
HAMWORTHY
POOLE
WEST BAY
Frampton Tunnel
MORETON
HOLTON HEATH
PARKSTONE
BOURNEMOUTH DEPOT
DORCHESTER WEST
Dorchester Jc.
DORCHESTER SOUTH
WOOL
WAREHAM
Worgret Junc.
ABBOTSBURY
Bincombe Tun.
FURZEBROOK
NORDEN
UPWEY
Swanage Railway
CORFE CASTLE

G

Weymouth Jc.
WEYMOUTH
WEYMOUTH QUAY
HARMAN'S CROSS
SWANAGE
HERSTON HALT
PORTLAND
EASTON

BRISTOL (inset)
Clifton Down Tunnel
CLIFTON DOWN
REDLAND
Montpelier Tunnel
MONTPELIER
Ashley Hill Jc.
STAPLETON RD
Kingswood Jc.
WAPPING WHARF
BARTON HILL
LAWRENCE HILL
Dr Days Bridge Jc.
Bristol Harbour Railway
Ashton Jc.
TEMPLE MEADS
Feeder Br. Jc.
PARSON ST
BEDMINSTER
Bristol West Jc.
St. Anne's Park Jc.
Parson St Jc.

5   Ten   4   3   2   1

A

MAIDENHEAD
WARGRAVE
TWYFORD
PANGBOURNE
TILEHURST
West Jc.
Westbury Line
Oxford Road Jc.
READING
READING WEST
Southcote Jc.
WINNERSH TRIANGLE
WINNERSH
EARLEY
WOKINGHAM
BRACKNELL
ASCOT
MARTINS HERON
THEALE
CROWTHORNE
BAGSHOT
HUNGERFORD
KINTBURY
NEWBURY RACECOURSE
ALDERMASTON
MORTIMER
SANDHURST
CAMBERLEY
BLACKWATER
FRIMLEY
Pirbright Jc.
MARLBOROUGH
Enbourne Jc.
NEWBURY
THATCHAM
MIDGHAM
FARNBOROUGH NORTH
FARNBOROUGH MAIN
NORTH CAMP
M. & S. W. Jc.
BEDWYN
BRAMLEY
HOOK
FLEET
WINCHFIELD
ALDERSHOT
ASH VALE
ASH Jc.
Wolfhall Jc.
Grafton Jc.
LUDGERSHALL
OVERTON
Worting Jc.
BASINGSTOKE
PEWSEY
WHITCHURCH
Farnham Jc.

B

ANDOVER
Red Posts Jc.
Litchfield Tun.
FARNHAM
BULFORD CAMP
Popham Tuns.
MICHELDEVER
BENTLEY
GRATELEY
ALTON
Butts Jc.
BORDON
Hindhead
Amesbury Jc.
Waller's Ash Tun.
MEDSTEAD & FOUR MARKS
HASLEMERE
Summit
Winchester Jc.
Mid Hants Railway
ROPLEY
LIPHOOK
Tunnel Jc.
SALISBURY
Fisherton Tun.
Laverstock Jc.
ALRESFORD
LISS
Alderbury Jc.
DEAN
WINCHESTER
PETERSFIELD
MIDHURST
DUNBRIDGE
Kimbridge Jc.
Shawford Jc.
SHAWFORD
Butser Hill
Buriton Tun.
Summit

C

D

ROMSEY
BISHOP'S WALTHAM
EASTLEIGH
Eastleigh S.Jc.
SOUTHAMPTON AIRPORT PARKWAY
SWAYTHLING
HEDGE END
ST.DENYS
TOTTON
REDBRIDGE
SOUTHAMPTON CENTRAL
BITTERNE
MILLBROOK
WOOLSTON
SHOLING
BOTLEY
Tapnage Tunnel
SOUTHAMPTON
SOUTHAMPTON EASTERN DOCKS
MARCHWOOD
NETLEY
BURSLEDON
ROWLANDS CASTLE
ASHURST NEW FOREST
HAMBLE
SWANWICK
BEDHAMPTON
WARBLINGTON
NUTBOURNE
BEAULIEU ROAD
FAREHAM
Farlington Junc
Cosham Jc.
HAVANT
EMSWORTH
BOSHAM
CHICHESTER
RINGWOOD
PORTCHESTER
COSHAM
Portcreek Jc.
SOUTHBOURNE
FISHBOURNE
BROCKENHURST
FAWLEY
HILSEA
Lymington Jc.
GOSPORT
PORTSMOUTH AND SOUTHSEA
SWAY
HARBOUR
FRATTON
HAYLING ISLAND
SELSEY

E

HINTON ADMIRAL
NEW MILTON
LYMINGTON TOWN
PIER
COWES
PORTSMOUTH
CHRISTCHURCH
POKESDOWN
NEWPORT
RYDE PIERHEAD
RYDE ESPLANADE
RYDE ST. JOHN'S ROAD
SMALLBROOK JUNCTION
YARMOUTH
WOOTTON
HAVEN ST
Isle of Wight Steam Railway
BEMBRIDGE
FRESHWATER
ASHEY
BRADING
ISLE OF WIGHT
LAKE
SANDOWN
SHANKLIN
St. Catherine's Down
VENTNOR
St. Boniface Down
VENTNOR TOWN

F

G

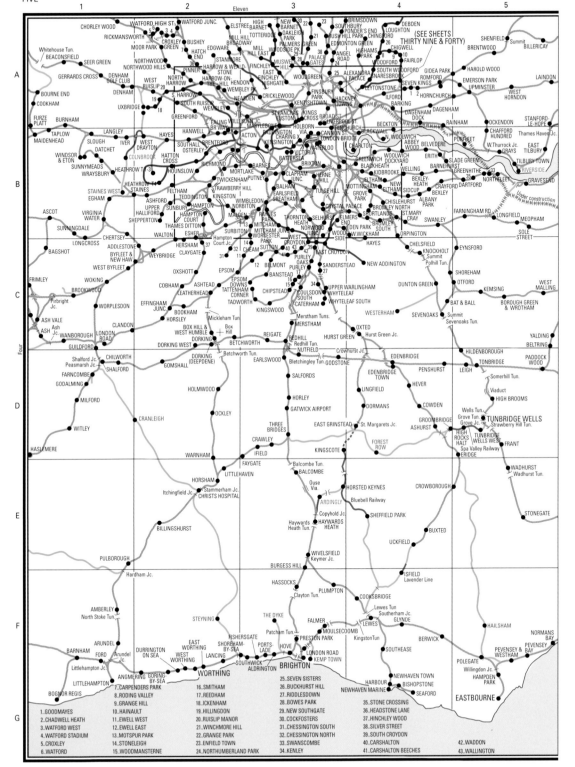

BATTLESBRIDGE
WOODHAM FERRERS
FAMBRIDGE
ALTHORPE
BURNHAM ON CROUCH
WICKFORD
HOCKLEY
ROCHFORD
RAYLEIGH
BASILDON
PITSEA
PRITTLEWELL
BENFLEET
LEIGH ON SEA
CHALKWELL
VICTORIA
THORPE BAY
Canvey Island
CENTRAL
WESTCLIFF
EAST
PIG'S BAY
SHOEBURYNESS
SOUTHEND-ON-SEA

A

THAMESHAVEN

Hoo Jc.
HIGHAM
PORT VICTORIA
SHEERNESS-ON-SEA
Higham Tnl.
Rochester Br. Jc.
Fort Pitt Tun.
THAMES PORT
QUEENBOROUGH
Strood Tnl.
STROOD
King's Ferry Bri.
LEYSDOWN
WESTGATE-ON-SEA
MARGATE
Gillingham Tun.
GILLINGHAM
RAINHAM
SWALE
CHESTFIELD & SWALECLIFFE
BIRCHINGTON-ON-SEA
BROADSTAIRS
DUMPTON PARK
Chatham Tun.
NEWINGTON
HERNE BAY
Minster West Jc.
RAMSGATE
CUXTON
CHATHAM
ROCHESTER
Western Jc.
KEMSLEY
SITTINGBOURNE
WHITSTABLE
MINSTER
Minster East Jc.

B

HALLING
SNODLAND
Eastern Jc.
TEYNHAM
STURRY
Minster South Jc.
SANDWICH ROAD
NEW HYTHE
FAVERSHAM
WEST
CANTERBURY
SANDWICH
AYLESFORD
Faversham Jc.
EAST
BEKESBOURNE
EAST MALLING
SELLING
WINGHAM
EAST BEARSTED
Selling Tun.
CHARTHAM
ADISHAM
DEAL
Preston Hall Tuns.
BARMING
BARRACKS WEST
HOLLINGBOURNE
CHILHAM
AYLESHAM
SNOWDOWN
EAST FARLEIGH
MAIDSTONE
HARRIETSHAM
LENHAM
EYTHORNE
WALMER
WATERINGBURY
East Kent Light R.

C

CHARING
WYE
SHEPHERDS WELL
MARTIN MILL
MARDEN
STAPLEHURST
Lydden Tun.
Guston Tun.
HEADCORN
PLUCKLEY
KEARSNEY
Buckland Jc.
Priory Tun.
Charlton Tun.
PRIORY
Saltwood Tun.
Shakespeare Tun.
Harb. Tun.
ASHFORD INTERNATIONAL
DOVER
Archcliffe Jc.
Abbotscliffe Tun.
WESTENHANGER
SANDLING
FOLKESTONE WEST
CENT.
Martello Tun.
Sandling Tun.
HARB.
FOLKESTONE
HAWKHURST
HYTHE
SANDGATE
To France

D

HAM STREET
TENTERDEN TOWN
ROLVENDEN
BURMARSH ROAD HALT (Schools only)
Kent & East Sussex Railway
APPLEDORE
DYMCHURCH
ETCHINGHAM
NORTHIAM
WITTERSHAM ROAD
ST MARYS BAY
Romney, Hythe & Dymchurch Railway
BODIAM
NEW ROMNEY & LITTLESTONE-ON-SEA
ROBERTSBRIDGE
RYE
NEW ROMNEY
Mountfield Tun.
Tramway
ROMNEY SANDS
WINCHELSEA
CAMBER
POWER STATION
DUNGENESS

E

HARBOUR
BATTLE
DOLEHAM
THREE OAKS
CROWHURST
Bopeep Tunnel
Ore Tun.
ORE
WEST ST LEONARDS
Mount Pleasant Tun.
BEXHILL
HASTINGS
COLLINGTON
Hastings Tun.
Bopeep Jc.
ST LEONARDS WARRIOR SQUARE
CODDEN BEACH

F

G

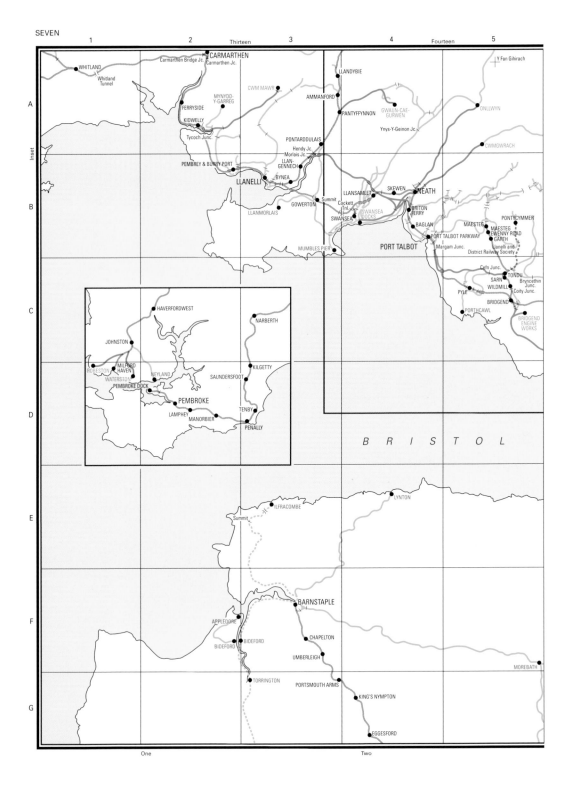

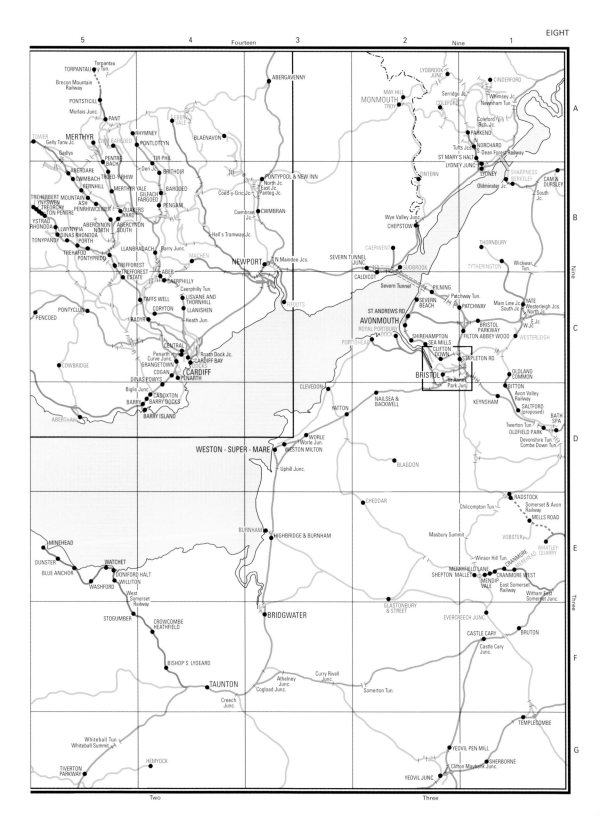

Titterstone Clee

HIGHLEY
Severn Valley Railway
ARLEY
NORTHWOOD HALT
CLEOBURY MORTIMER
STOURBRIDGE TOWN
LYE
STOURBRIDGE JC.
HAGLEY
BLAKEDOWN
KIDDERMINSTER TOWN
KIDDERMINSTER
HALESOWEN
HARBORNE
BOURNVILLE
KING'S NORTON
SELLY OAK
SPRING ROAD
ACOCKS GREEN
BOLTON
HALL GREEN
HAMPTON-IN-ARDEN
SOLIHULL
YARDLEY WOOD
SHIRLEY
WIDNEY MANOR
BERKSWELL

LUDLOW
CLEE HILL
BEWDLEY
Halesowen Jc.
LONGBRIDGE (ROVER)
NORTHFIELD
LONGBRIDGE
WHITLOCK'S END
EARLSWOOD
WYTHALL
THE LAKES
DORRIDGE
LAPWORTH

A

STOURPORT
HARTLEBURY
Summit
BARNT GREEN
WOOD END
Wood End Tunnel
DANZEY
Lickey Incline
ALVECHURCH
BROMSGROVE
REDDITCH

HENLEY-IN-ARDEN
N. Jc.
E.Jc.
HATTON
S.Jc.
CLAVERDON

LEOMINSTER
BROMYARD
DROITWICH SPA
Stoke Works Jc.
WOOTTON WAWEN
N.Jc.
BEARLEY
E.Jc.
W.Jc.
ALCESTER
WILMCOTE

B

Rainbow Hill Tunnel
Tunnel Jc.
Rainbow Hill Jc.
WORCESTER
Leominster Jc.
FOREGATE ST.
SHRUB HILL
Norton Jc.
STRATFORD-ON-AVON

Dinmore Tun.
Abbotswood Jc.

Brecon Curve Jc.
Barrs Ct .Jc. N.
Shelwick Jc.
MALVERN LINK
GREAT MALVERN
Malvern Jc.
PERSHORE
LONG MARSTON

Fourteen

MOORFIELDS
Barrs Ct Jc. 3
HEREFORD
Rotherwas Jc.
COLWALL
EVESHAM
HONEYBOURNE
Campden Tun.

Red Hill Jc.
LEDBURY
SHIPSTON-ON-STOUR

C

TEWKESBURY
ASHCHURCH FOR TEWKESBURY
GRETTON MEADOW
Greet Tun.
TODDINGTON
MORETON-IN-MARSH
Summit

NEWENT
GOTHERINGTON (proposed)
WINCHCOMBE
Gloucestershire Warwickshire Railway
CHELTENHAM RACECOURSE (proposed)

D

ROSS-ON-WYE
Hunting Butts Tun.
Honeybourne Line Jc.
Banbury Line Jc.
CHELTENHAM SPA
ANDOVERSFORD
KINGHAM

Over Jc.
GLOUCESTER
Hatherley Curve Jc.

LYDBROOK JUNC.
Docks
Engine Shed Jc.
Level Crossing

MAY HILL
CINDERFORD
Bilson Jc.
Serridge Jc.
Whimsey Jc.
Newnham Tunnel
Tuffley Jc.

MONMOUTH TROY
COLEFORD
Docks
Standish Jc.

E

Coleford Bch Jc.
PARKEND
Dean Forest Railway
Tufts Jcs.
NORCHARD N.
S.
ST MARY'S HALT
LYDNEY JUN.
STONEHOUSE
STROUD

LYDNEY
Docks
Oldminster Jc.
SHARPNESS
BERKELEY
CAM & DURSLEY
Viaduct
CIRENCESTER
Sapperton Tun.
Summit
FAIRFORD

South Jc.
DURSLEY
NAILSWORTH
KEMBLE
Kemble Tunnel

F

Wye Valley Junc.
CHEPSTOW
THORNBURY
TETBURY
CRICKLADE
HIGHWORTH

CAERWENT
SEVERN TUNNEL JC.
SUDBROOK
TYTHERINGTON
Wickwar Tun.
Swindon & Cricklade Railway
BLUNSDON
STRATTON (ROVER GROUP)

CALDICOT
MALMESBURY
SWINDON (MOREDON)

Severn Tunnel
SEVERN BEACH
PILNING
YATE
Westerleigh Jcs.
Alderton Tun.
Wootton Bassett Jc.
Highworth Jc.
SWINDON

ST ANDREW'S ROAD
PATCHWAY
Main Line South Jc
Westerleigh North Jc.
E.Jc.
Chipping Sodbury Tun.
Rushey Platt Jc.

ROYAL PORTBURY DOCK
AVONMOUTH
SHIREHAMPTON
BRISTOL PARKWAY
W.Jc.

PORTISHEAD
SEA MILLS
CLIFTON DOWN
FILTON ABBEY WOOD
WESTERLEIGH

G

5   Sixteen   4   3   2   1

Beechwood Tun.
COVENTRY
Humber Rd.Jc.
TILE HILL
CANLEY
Kenilworth Jc.
Glendon S.Jc.
KETTERING
Kettering Jc.
THRAPSTON

A

WARWICK PARKWAY
Marton Jc.
WARWICK
LEAMINGTON SPA
RUGBY
Kilsby Tun.
Crick Tun.
Watford Lodge Tun.
LONG BUCKBY
PITSFORD
Northampton & Lamport Railway
WELLINGBOROUGH
Irchester Jc.
Sharnbrook Tun.
Sharnbrook Summit

B

KINETON
Fenny Compton Jc.
Catesby Tun.
Woodford Jc.
Stowe Hill Tun.
Hunsbury Hill Tun.
NORTHAMPTON
BRACKMILLS
BRIDGE STREET
Ravenstone Wood Jc.
Roade Jc.
Oakley Jc.
Bedford N.Jc.
BEDFORD
Kempston Rd Jc.
BEDFORD ST JOHNS

Culworth Jc.
TOWCESTER
NEWPORT PAGNELL
KEMPSTON HARDWICK
STEWARTBY
MILLBROOK

C

Banbury Jc.
BANBURY
Cockley Brake Jc.
BRACKLEY
WOLVERTON
MILTON KEYNES CENTRAL
LIDLINGTON
ASPLEY GUISE
RIDGMONT
Ampthill Tun.
KING'S SUTTON
Aynho Jc.
BUCKINGHAM
BLETCHLEY
WOBURN SANDS
BOW BRICKHILL
FENNY STRATFORD
FLITWICK

CHIPPING NORTON
Ardley Tunnel
Claydon LNE Junction
HARLINGTON
STONEHENGE WORKS
Leighton Buzzard Railway

D

HEYFORD
NORTH BICESTER TOWN
Grendon Underwood Jc.
Quainton Rd.Jc.
Linslade Tuns.
LEIGHTON BUZZARD
PAGES PARK
DUNSTABLE
LEAGRAVE
SHIPTON
CHARLBURY
TACKLEY
ASCOTT-UNDER-WYCHWOOD
FINSTOCK
Bicester Military Railway
Q & A Tramroad
QUAINTON ROAD
CHEDDINGTON
COMBE
HANBOROUGH
ISLIP
Ashendon Jcs.
North Jc.
AYLESBURY
South Jc.
TRING

E

Witney Jc.
Oxford Rd. Jc.
Wolvercot Jc.
Chearsley Viaduct
HADDENHAM AND THAME PARKWAY
STOKE MANDEVILLE
WENDOVER
Northchurch Tun.
BERKHAMSTED
OXFORD
COWLEY
THAME
LITTLE KIMBLE
MONKS RISBOROUGH
Summit
HEMEL HEMPSTEAD
APSLEY
Kennington Jc.

F

RADLEY
ABINGDON
WAINHILL (restored but not open)
Chinnor & Princes Risborough Railway
CHINNOR
PRINCES RISBOROUGH
GREAT MISSENDEN
CHESHAM
KING'S LANGLEY
Summit
CHALFONT & LATIMER
FARINGDON
CULHAM
APPLEFORD
Viaduct
Didcot N.Jc.
WATLINGTON
SAUNDERTON
AMERSHAM
CHORLEYWOOD
Foxhall Jc.
Didcot W.Curve Jc.
DIDCOT PARKWAY
Didcot E.Jc.
HIGH WYCOMBE
RICKMANSWORTH
Tramway
WANTAGE
WALLINGFORD
Cholsey & Wallingford Railway
BEACONSFIELD
White House Farm Tun.
SEER GREEN
GERRARDS CROSS
DENHAM

G

CHOLSEY
MARLOW
BOURNE END
COOKHAM
DENHAM GOLF CLUB
WEST RUISLIP
LAMBOURN
GORING & STREATLEY
HENLEY-ON-THAMES
SHIPLAKE
FURZE PLATT
TAPLOW
BURNHAM
SLOUGH
UXBRIDGE
IVER
LANGLEY
WEST DRAYTON
PANGBOURNE
WARGRAVE
MAIDENHEAD
WINDSOR & ETON CENTRAL
WINDSOR & ETON RIVERSIDE
DATCHET
COLNBROOK
TILEHURST
TWYFORD

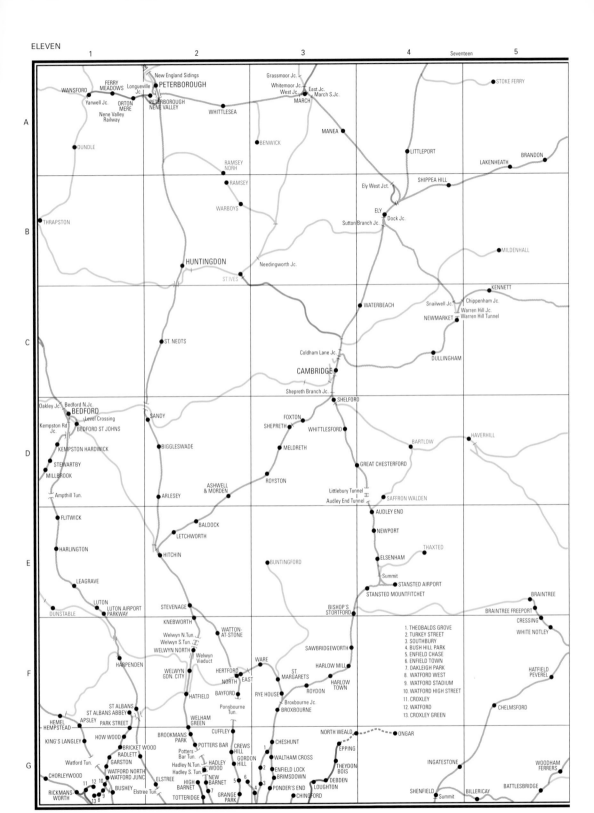

1. THEOBALDS GROVE
2. TURKEY STREET
3. SOUTHBURY
4. BUSH HILL PARK
5. ENFIELD CHASE
6. ENFIELD TOWN
7. OAKLEIGH PARK
8. WATFORD WEST
9. WATFORD STADIUM
10. WATFORD HIGH STREET
11. CROXLEY
12. WATFORD
13. CROXLEY GREEN

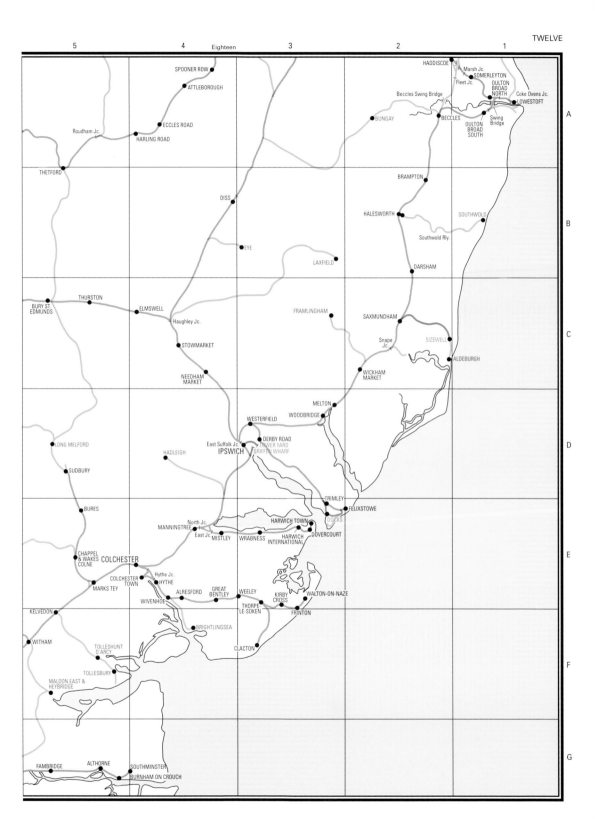

SPOONER ROW
ATTLEBOROUGH
HADDISCOE
Marsh Jc.
SOMERLEYTON
Fleet Jc.
OULTON
BROAD
NORTH
Beccles Swing Bridge
Coke Ovens Jc.
LOWESTOFT
ECCLES ROAD
Roudham Jc.
BUNGAY
BECCLES
Swing
Bridge
HARLING ROAD
OULTON
BROAD
SOUTH
A

THETFORD
BRAMPTON
DISS
HALESWORTH
SOUTHWOLD
B
EYE
Southwold Rly.
LAXFIELD
DARSHAM

THURSTON
BURY ST.
EDMUNDS
ELMSWELL
FRAMLINGHAM
SAXMUNDHAM
C
Haughley Jc.
SIZEWELL
STOWMARKET
Snape
Jc.
ALDEBURGH
NEEDHAM
MARKET
WICKHAM
MARKET

MELTON
WESTERFIELD
WOODBRIDGE
LONG MELFORD
East Suffolk Jc.
DERBY ROAD
LOWER YARD
D
HADLEIGH
IPSWICH
GRIFFEN WHARF
SUDBURY

TRIMLEY
BURES
FELIXSTOWE
North Jc.
MANNINGTREE
HARWICH TOWN
DOCKS
E
CHAPPEL
& WAKES
COLNE
COLCHESTER
East Jc.
MISTLEY
WRABNESS
DOVERCOURT
HARWICH
INTERNATIONAL
Hythe Jc.
COLCHESTER
TOWN
HYTHE
ALRESFORD
GREAT
BENTLEY
WEELEY
KIRBY
CROSS
WALTON-ON-NAZE
MARKS TEY
WIVENHOE
THORPE
LE-SOKEN
FRINTON
KELVEDON
BRIGHTLINGSEA
WITHAM
TOLLESHUNT
D'ARCY
CLACTON
F
TOLLESBURY
MALDON EAST &
HEYBRIDGE

FAMBRIDGE
ALTHORNE
SOUTHMINSTER
G
BURNHAM ON CROUCH

1   2   3   4   5

A

B

C

D

E

F

G

BIRMINGHAM DISTRICT
(INSET ON SHEET No. FIFTEEN)

PRIESTFIELD
THE CRESCENT
BILSTON CENTRAL
LOXDALE
BRADLEY LANE
COSELEY
WEDNESBURY PARKWAY
Goods Branch Jc.
Darlaston Jc.
Pleck Jc.
East Jc.
West Jc.
South Jc.
WEDNESBURY GREAT WESTERN STREET
BESCOT STADIUM
TAME BRIDGE PARKWAY
HAMSTEAD
Horsleyfield Jc.
TIPTON
Hill Top Tunnel
BLACK LAKE
DUDLEY ST/ GUNS VILLAGE
DUDLEY PORT
LODGE ROAD
WEST BROMWICH TOWN HALL
WEST BROMWICH CENTRAL
Perry Barr North Jc.
Sedgley Jc.
DARTMOUTH STREET
KENRICK PARK
Perry Barr West Jc.
GRAVELLY HILL
WITTON
DUDLEY
SANDWELL & DUDLEY
TRINITY WAY
Handsworth Jc.
PERRY BARR
OLDBURY
THE HAWTHORNS
SMETHWICK GALTON BRIDGE
HANDSWORTH BOOTH ST.
Soho Pool Jc.
ASTON
SMETHWICK ROLFE ST.
WINSON GREEN OUTER CIRCLE
Galton Jc.
SOHO BENSON ROAD
DUDDESTON
LANGLEY GREEN
Soho Soap Works Jc.
Soho East Jc.
JEWELLERY QUARTER
Landor Street Jc.
Hockley Tunnel
ST PAULS
Harborne Jc.
SNOW HILL
LAWLEY STR.
ADDERLEY PARK
ABERYSTWYTH
OLD HILL
ROWLEY REGIS
Old Hill Tunnel
Proof House Jc.
New Street North Tunnel
NEW ST.
Curzon Str.Jc.
St. Andrew's Jc.
FIVE WAYS
MOOR ST.
BORDESLEY
Bordesley Jc.
GLANRAFON
LLANBADARN
Vale of Rheidol
CAPEL BANGOR
HARBORNE
UNIVERSITY
Camp Hill Jc.

DYFFRYN ARDUDWY
TALYBONT
LLANABER
Barmouth Bridge
BARMOUTH
MORFA MAWDDACH
FAIRBOURNE
Cader Idris
LLWYNGWRIL
ABERGYNOLWYN
DOLGOCH FALLS
TONFANAU
Talyllyn
BRYNGLAS
RHYDYRONEN
PENDRE
WHARF STA.
TYWYN
ABERDOVEY
PENHELIG
BORTH

ABERAYRON

Aberayron Jc.
LAMPETER

CARDIGAN

FISHGUARD HARBOUR

PONTPRENSHITW
LLANDYFRIOG
FOREST HALT
HENLLAN
NEWCASTLE EMLYN
Teifi Valley Railway

Letterston Jc.
TRECWN

CYNWYL ELFED (proposed)
DANYCOED
LLWYFAN CERRIG
Gwili Railway
BRONWYDD ARMS
LLANDEILO

Spittal Tun.
Clarbeston Jc.
CLARBESTON ROAD
CLUNDERWEN
Carmarthen Bridge Jc.
CARMARTHEN
Carmarthen Jc.
FFAIRFACH

WHITLAND

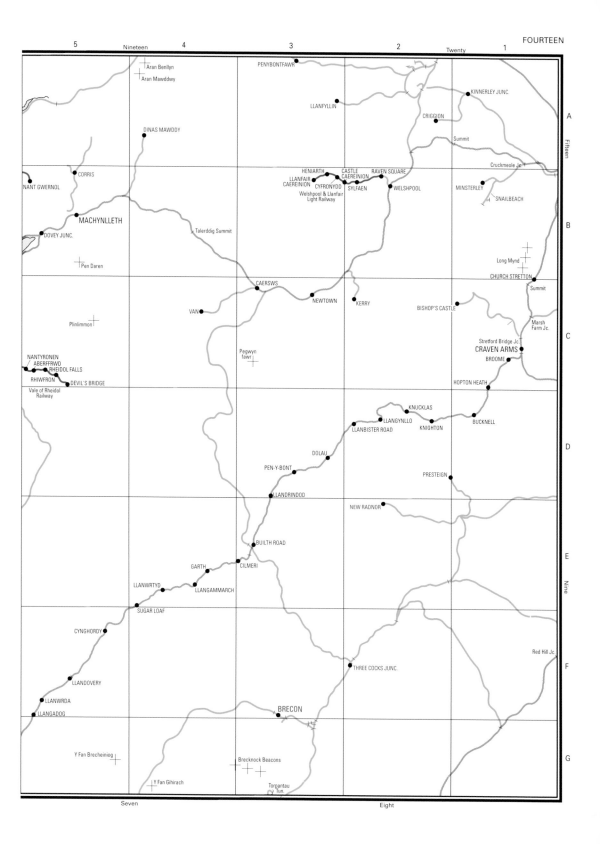

Aran Benllyn
Aran Mawddwy
PENYBONTFAWR
KINNERLEY JUNC.
LLANFYLLIN
CRIGGION
A
DINAS MAWDDY
Summit
Fifteen
CORRIS
Cruckmeole Jc.
HENIARTH   CASTLE
NANT GWERNOL
LLANFAIR   CAEREINION   RAVEN SQUARE
CAEREINION   CYFRONYDD   SYLFAEN
MINSTERLEY
DOVEY JUNC.
Welshpool   WELSHPOOL
SNAILBEACH
MACHYNLLETH
Welshpool & Llanfair
Light Railway
B
Talerddig Summit
Pen Daren
Long Mynd
CHURCH STRETTON
CAERSWS
Summit
NEWTOWN
KERRY
Plinlimmon
VAN
BISHOP'S CASTLE
Marsh
Farm Jc.
Pegwyn
fawr
Stretford Bridge Jc.
CRAVEN ARMS
NANTYRONEN
BROOME
ABERFFRWD
RHEIDOL FALLS
RHIWFRON
HOPTON HEATH
DEVIL'S BRIDGE
Vale of Rheidol
Railway
KNUCKLAS
LLANGYNLLO   BUCKNELL
LLANBISTER ROAD   KNIGHTON
C
DOLAU
PEN-Y-BONT
PRESTEIGN
D
LLANDRINDOD
NEW RADNOR
BUILTH ROAD
GARTH   CILMERI
E
LLANWRTYD
Nine
LLANGAMMARCH
SUGAR LOAF
CYNGHORDY
Red Hill Jc.
THREE COCKS JUNC.
F
LLANDOVERY
LLANWRDA
BRECON
LLANGADOG
Y Fan Brecheiniog
G
Brecknock Beacons
Y Fan Gihirach
Torpantau
Tun.

1 2 Twenty 3 4 Twenty one 5

A

HOUGH GN
Widnes Jc.
WARRINGTON
CATCHFORD
ALTRINCHAM
CHEADLE HULME
DAVENPORT
HAZEL GROVE
STRINES
HAYFIELD
The Peak
WIDNES
FIDDLERS FERRY
HALE
HEALD GREEN
WOODSMOOR
MIDDLEWOOD
Cowburn Tun.
HALEWOOD
Acton Grange Jc.
ASHLEY
MANCHESTER AIRPORT
STYAL
BRAMHALL
POYNTON
Disley Tunnel
NEW MILLS CENTRAL
NEW MILLS NEWTOWN
EDALE
HOPE
BAMFORD
TANHOUSE LANE
RUNCORN
(SEE SHEET NO.FORTY FIVE)
HANDFORTH
DISLEY
CHINLEY
ICI WORKS
Sutton Tun.
RUNCORN EAST
MOBBERLEY
WILMSLOW
FURNESS VALE
WHALEY BRIDGE
N.Jc.
Chinley E.Jc.
Mam Tor
HATHERSAGE
Halton Jc.
ADLINGTON
CHAPEL-EN-LE-FRITH
Frodsham Jc.
KNUTSFORD
ALDERLEY EDGE
Prestbury Tun.
PRESTBURY
Dove Holes Tun.
Summit
INCE & ELTON
HELSBY
Weaver Jc.
WINNINGTON
PLUMLEY
CHELFORD
Hibel Rd Tunnel
DOVE HOLES
PEAK FOREST
Litton Tun.
Cressbrook Tun.
ACTON BRIDGE
GREENBANK
LOSTOCK GRALAM
NORTHWICH
BUXTON
Miller's Dale Jc.
Chee Tor Tuns.
Headstone Tun.
CUDDINGTON
HARTFORD
MACCLESFIELD
Summit
HINDLOW
MOULDS WORTH
DELAMERE
GOOSTREY
Winsford Jc.
Hadden Tun.
Mickle Trafford Jc.
HOLMES CHAPEL
WINSFORD

B

Christleton Tun.
Tattenhall Jc.
SANDBACH
CONGLETON
Upper Jc.
LEEK
HULME END

C

Crewe North Jc.
N.S. Jc.
ALSAGER
KIDSGROVE
Leek Brook Jc.
WATERHOUSES
Manchester Line Jc.
Gresty Lane Jc.
CREWE
Harecastle Tun.
Cheddleton Tun.
CHEDDLETON
NANTWICH
Basford Hall Jc.
Jamage Jc.
CONSALL
Churnet Valley Railway
CALDON LOW
Market Drayton Jc.
Diglake Jc.
LONGPORT
KINGSLEY & FROGHALL
WRENBURY
ETRURIA
Botteslow Jc.
OAKAMOOR
Stretton Jc.
Wetmore Jc.
North Jc.
Summit
STOKE
LONGTON
Meir Tunnel
CHEADLE
N.Staff. Jc.
WHITCHURCH
Summit
BLYTHE BRIDGE
Horninglow Jc.
South Jc.
WEDGEWOOD
Guild Str. Jc.

D

BARLASTON
BURTON-ON-TRENT
MARKET DRAYTON
STONE
Leicester Jc.
PREES
NORTON BRIDGE
UTTOXETER
TUTBURY & HATTON
Marston Jc.
Dove Jc.
WEM
Stretton Jc.
BURTON-ON-TRENT
YORTON
(SEE INSET)
Leicester Jc.
STAFFORD
Branston Jc.

E

Trent Valley Jc.
West Jc.
RUGELEY (T.V.)
Wichnor Jc.
Birmingham Curve Jc.
NEWPORT
Bushbury Jc.
Shugborough Tun.
East Jc.
RUGELEY TOWN
HEDNESFORD
English Bridge Jc.
SHREWSBURY
Abbey Foregate Jc.
Stafford Jc.
OAKENGATES
WOLVERHAMPTON
WOLVERHAMPTON ST GEORGES
Heath Town Jc.
Crane St. Jc.
PENKRIDGE
LICHFIELD
TRENT VALLEY
WELLINGTON
Ketley Jc.
TELFORD CENTRAL
THE ROYAL
PRIESTFIELD
CANNOCK
CITY
The Wrekin
Madeley Jc.

F

SHIFNAL
LANDYWOOD
BROWNHILLS
SHENSTONE
IRONBRIDGE POWER STATION
COSFORD
BLOXWICH NORTH
TAMWORTH
ALBRIGHTON
CODSALL
BLOXWICH
WILNECOTE
BILBROOK
Bushbury Jc.
BLAKE STR.
BUTLERS LANE
FOUR OAKS
BADDESLEY
COALPORT
MUCH WENLOCK
Ryecroft Jc.
WALSALL
SUTTON COLDFIELD
Caer Caradoc
WOLVERHAMPTON
BESCOT STADIUM
TAME BRIDGE PARKWAY
WYLDE GREEN
CHESTER RD
WATER ORTON
Kingsbury Jc.
CHURCH STRETTON
(SEE INSET ON SHEET NO THIRTEEN)
HAMSTEAD
PERRY BARR
ERDINGTON
Whitacre Jc.
BRIDGNORTH

G

DITTON PRIORS
Severn Valley Railway
SHUT END
ROUND OAK
OLDBURY
GRAVELLY HILL
BIRMINGHAM
ADDERLEY PARK
COLESHILL
Marsh Farm Jc.
Brown Clee
HAMPTON LOADE
LANGLEY GREEN
ROWLEY REGIS
ASTON
SNOW HILL
STECHFORD
LEA HALL
CRADLEY HEATH
FIVE WAYS
UNIVERSITY
NEW STREET
BORDESLEY
SMALLHEATH
TYSELEY
MARSTON GREEN
BIRMINGHAM INTERNATIONAL
COUNTRY PARK HALT
STOURBRIDGE TOWN
LYE
HALESOWEN
OLD HILL
HARBORNE
SELLY OAK
SPRING ROAD
ACOCKS GREEN
OLTON
HAMPTON-IN-ARDEN
HIGHLEY
STOURBRIDGE JC.
BOURNVILLE
HALL GREEN

Nine

Twenty

Fourteen

5   Twenty one   4   3   Twenty two   2   1

South Yorkshire Supertram
SHEFFIELD
DARNALL
GLEADLESS
TOWNSEND
WOODHOUSE
Treeton Jc.
Southern Jc.
KIVETON
BRIDGE
Dimington Jc.
GAINSBOROUGH
CENTRAL
GAINSBOROUGH
LEA ROAD
HERDINGS PARK
KIVETON
PARK
G.C. & Mid.Jc.
SHIREOAKS
DORE
Dore S.Jc.
Bradway Tun.
DRONFIELD
HALFWAY
Brancliffe Jc.
WORKSOP
Clarborough Jc.
North Jc.
RETFORD
South Jc.
Clarborough
Tun.
Pyewipe Jc.
W.Holmes Jc.
LINCOLN
CENTRAL
Totley Tun.
Whisker Hill Jc.
Boultham
Jc.
Sincil Jc.
GRINDLEFORD
Broomhouse Tun.
WHITWELL
Askham Tun.
COTTAM
Sykes Jc.
West
Holmes Jc.
LINCOLN
CHESTERFIELD
Tapton Jc.
OXCROFT
CRESWELL
SAXILBY
Pyewipe Jc.
Durham Ox. Jc.
ROWSLEY SOUTH
Peak Rail
BOLSOVER
LANGWITH-
WHALEY THORNS
WELBECK COLLIERY
HIGH
MARNHAM
Boultham Jc.
LINCOLN CENTRAL
Sincil Jc.
Great-
well Jcs.
DARLEY DALE
Clay Cross Tunnel
SHIREBROOK
HYKEHAM
MATLOCK
RIVERSIDE
MATLOCK
High Tor Tnls.
MATLOCK BATH
CLIPSTONE
COLLIERY
Clipstone Jc.
SWINDERBY
METHERINGHAM
Willersley Tun.
CROMFORD
Lea Wood Tun.
MANSFIELD
WOODHOUSE
MANSFIELD
COLLINGHAM
WIRKS
WORTH
High Peak Jc.
ALFRETON
SUTTON PARKWAY
KIRKBY-IN-
ASHFIELD
RUFFORD
COLLIERY
WHATSTAND
WELL
Wingfield
Tun.
Alfreton
Tun.
SOUTHWELL
Level Crossing
NEWARK CASTLE
West Jc.
AMBERGATE
South Jc.
East Jc.
BUTTERLEY
Midland Railway
Centre
NEWSTEAD
HUCKNALL
CALVERTON
COLLIERY
FISKERTON
BLEASBY
THURGARTON
ROLLESTON
NEWARK NORTH GATE
BELPER
DENBY
Moorbridge Jc.
LOWDHAM
Barkston
East Jc.
ANCASTER
SLEAFORD
Milford Tun.
LANGLEY MILL
BULWELL
Leen Valley Jc.
BURTON JOYCE
Barkston South Jc.
RAUCEBY
DUFFIELD
PHOENIX PARK
GEDLING
Saxondale Jc.
ELTON
& ORSTON
W.Jc.
N.Jc.
Little Eaton Jc.
Trowell Jc.
CARLTON
BINGHAM
ASLOCKTON
E.Jc.
Belvoir Jc.
BOTTESFORD
Peascliffe Tun.
Derby N Jc.
Spondon Jc.
SPONDON
Rectory Jc.
NOTTINGHAM
RADCLIFFE
S. Jc.
Canal Yard
Nottingham Branch Jc.
GRANTHAM
DERBY
London
Road Jc.
BEESTON
ATTENBOROUGH
PEARTREE
Attenborough Jc.
RUDDINGTON
TOLLERTON
East Jc.
Stenson Jc.
North Stafford Jc.
LONG EATON
Long Eaton Jc.
Sheet Stores Jc.
RUDDINGTON
Stoke
Tun.
WILLINGTON
SINFIN
Trent Jc.
Gotham Jc.
Stanton Tun.
Summit
Great Central Railway
(Nottingham) Ltd
Test Track
EAST
LEAKE
OLD DALBY
Wycombe Jc.
LOUGHBOROUGH
Saxelby Tun.
Wymondham Jc.
LOUGHBOROUGH
CENTRAL
BARROW UPON SOAR
MELTON
MOWBRAY
Melton Jc.
Wymondham Jc.
Seventeen
QUORN
& WOODHOUSE
SILEBY
Asfordby Tun.
Great Central
Railway
ROTHLEY
Syston
N.Jc.
Syston E. Jc.
Syston S. Jc.
SYSTON
LEICESTER NORTH
Glenfield
Tun.
N.
W.
S.
Morefield Jcs.
OAKHAM
POLESWORTH
SHACKERSTONE
MARKET
BOSWORTH
LEICESTER
Manton Tun.
STAMFORD
Battlefield Steam
Railway
SHENTON
Knighton Tun.
Knighton N.Jc.
Leicester Goods Jc.
Wing Tun.
Glaston Tun.
ATHERSTONE
NARBOROUGH
Knighton
S.Jc.
SOUTH WIGSTON
Wigston N.Jc.
Central Jc.
Wigston S.Jc.
Seaton Tun.
Weddington Jc.
HINCKLEY
Summit
Welland Viaduct
NUNEATON
S Leicester Jc.
Summit
Arley Tnl.
Kibworth Summit
Hallaton Jc.
Drayton Jc.
Corby Tun.
CORBY-CORUS WORKS
Welham Jc.
Summit
BEDWORTH
MARKET HARBOROUGH
Desborough Summit
Glendon S.Jc.

Ten

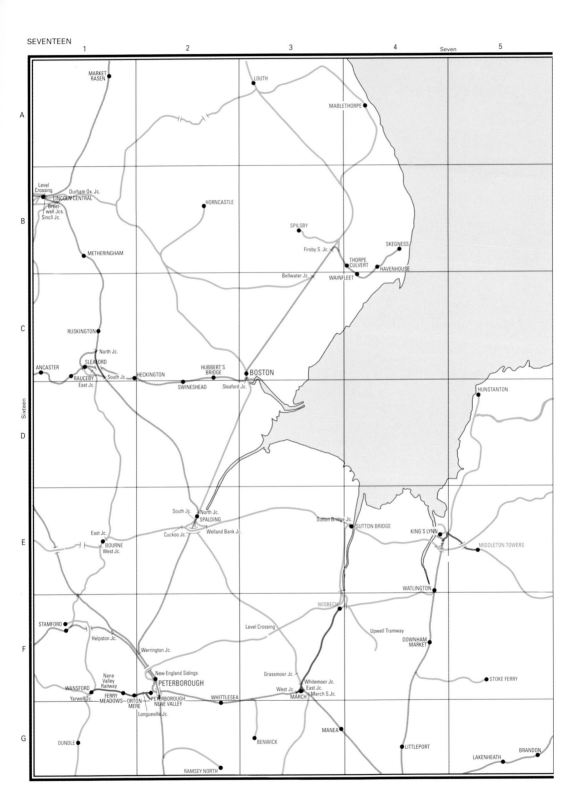

1   2   3   4   5

A

MARKET RASEN

LOUTH

MABLETHORPE

Level Crossing   Durham Ox. Jc.

B   LINCOLN CENTRAL

Greet-well Jcs.

Sincil Jc.

HORNCASTLE

SPILSBY

SKEGNESS

Firsby S. Jc.

THORPE CULVERT

HAVENHOUSE

METHERINGHAM

Bellwater Jc.

WAINFLEET

Sixteen

C

RUSKINGTON

North Jc.

SLEAFORD

HUBBERT'S BRIDGE

BOSTON

ANCASTER

RAUCEBY   South Jc.   HECKINGTON

HUNSTANTON

East Jc.   SWINESHEAD   Sleaford Jc.

D

E

South Jc.   North Jc.

SPALDING

Sutton Bridge Jc.

SUTTON BRIDGE

KING'S LYNN

East Jc.   Cuckoo Jc.   Welland Bank Jc.

MIDDLETON TOWERS

BOURNE

West Jc.

WATLINGTON

F

WISBECH

STAMFORD

Level Crossing

Upwell Tramway

DOWNHAM MARKET

Helpston Jc.

Werrington Jc.

Nene Valley Railway   New England Sidings

Grassmoor Jc.

STOKE FERRY

WANSFORD   PETERBOROUGH

Whitemoor Jc.

West Jc.   East Jc.

Yarwell Jc.   FERRY MEADOWS   ORTON MERE

PETERBOROUGH NENE VALLEY

WHITTLESEA

MARCH   March S. Jc.

Longueville Jc.

G

OUNDLE

BENWICK

MANEA

LITTLEPORT

BRANDON

RAMSEY NORTH

LAKENHEATH

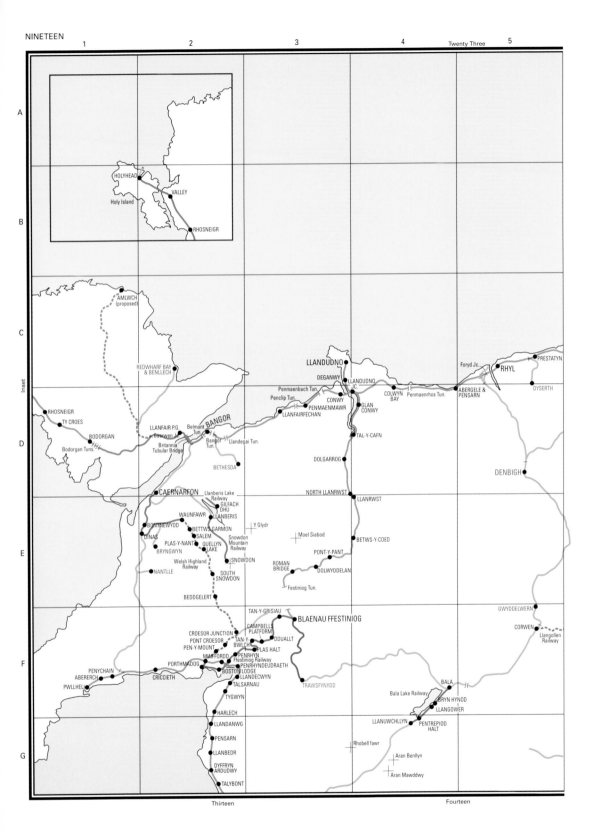

1   2   3   4   5

A

B

HOLYHEAD

VALLEY

Holy Island

RHOSNEIGR

Inset

C

AMLWCH
(proposed)

REDWHARF BAY
& BENLLECH

LLANDUDNO

DEGANWY
LLANDUDNO
JC.
Penmaenbach Tun.
Penclip Tun.
CONWY
GLAN
CONWY
COLWYN
BAY
Penmaenrhos Tun.

Foryd Jc.
RHYL
PRESTATYN

ABERGELE &
PENSARN

DYSERTH

RHOSNEIGR
TY CROES
BODORGAN
Bodorgan Tuns.

LLANFAIR P.G.
Gaerwen Jc.
Belmont
Tun.
BANGOR
Britannia
Tubular Bridge
Bangor
Tun.
Llandegai Tun.
PENMAENMAWR
LLANFAIRFECHAN

TAL-Y-CAFN

DOLGARROG

BETHESDA

CAERNARFON

Llanberis Lake
Railway
GILFACH
DHU
LLANBERIS
WAUNFAWR
BETTWS GARMON
SALEM
Snowdon
Mountain
Railway
Y Glydr
Moel Siabod

NORTH LLANRWST
LLANRWST

DENBIGH

BONTNEWYDD
DINAS
PLAS-Y-NANT
QUELLYN
LAKE
BRYNGWYN
Welsh Highland
Railway
SNOWDON
SOUTH
SNOWDON
ROMAN
BRIDGE
Festiniog Tun.
BETWS-Y-COED
PONT-Y-PANT
DOLWYDDELAN

NANTLLE

BEDDGELERT

TAN-Y-GRISIAU
CAMPBELLS
PLATFORM
BLAENAU FFESTINIOG
GWYDDELWERN

CORWEN
Llangollen
Railway

CROESOR JUNCTION
PONT CROESOR
PEN-Y-MOUNT
TAN-Y-
BWLCH
DDUALLT
PLAS HALT
PORTHMADOG
MINFFORDD
PENRHYN
Ffestiniog Railway
PENRHYNDEUDRAETH
PENYCHAIN
ABERERCH
CRICCIETH
BOSTON LODGE
LLANDECWYN
TALSARNAU
BALA
PWLLHELI
TYGWYN
TRAWSFYNYDD
Bala Lake Railway
BRYN HYNOD
LLANGOWER
HARLECH
LLANDANWG
PENSARN
LLANBEDR
DYFFRYN
ARDUDWY
TALYBONT
LLANUWCHLLYN
PENTREPIOD
HALT
Rhobell fawr
Aran Benllyn
Aran Mawddwy

G

ANSDELL & FAIRHAVEN   LYTHA M   Penwortham Jc.   MILL HILL   BLACKBURN
Kitson Wood Tun.   TODMORDEN
LOSTOCK HALL   BAMBER BRI.   PLEASINGTON   CHERRY TREE   Hoddlesden Jc.
East Jc.   HASLINGDEN   RAWTENSTALL   BACUP
LEYLAND N.U. Jc.   DARWEN   IRWELL VALE
Euxton Jc.

SOUTHPORT   CROSTON   EUXTON BALSHAW LANE   CHORLEY   ENTWISTLE   RAMSBOTTOM   SUMMERSEAT   SMITHY BR.
L.U. Jt.   Sough Tun.   HOLCOMBE BROOK   East Lancashire Railway   ROCHDALE
MEOLS COP   RUFFORD   ADLINGTON   HALL I' TH' WOOD   BROMLEY CROSS   BOLTON ST INTERCHANGE   MILN ROW
BIRKDALE   BESCAR LANE   NEW LANE   HORWICH   BURY   CASTLE-TON
HILLSIDE   BURSCOUGH BRI.   HOSCAR   PARBOLD   Standish Jc.   HORWICH PARKWAY   BOLTON   HOLLINWOOD   OLDHAM WERNETH
AINSDALE   BURSCOUGH JUNC.   APPLEY BRI.   BLACKROD   LOSTOCK   HEYWOOD   MIDDLETON   MOSTON   FAILSWORTH
FRESHFIELD   ORMSKIRK   AUGHTON PARK   GATHURST   Whelley Jc.   WESTHOUGHTON   MOSES GATE   RADCLIFFE   WHITEFIELD   MILLS HILL   HEATON PK   DEAN LANE
FORMBY   Hillhouse Jc.   TOWN GREEN   UPHOLLAND   ORRELL   WIGAN   DAISY HILL   FARNWORTH   KEARSLEY   PRESTWICH   CRUMPSALL
HIGHTOWN   Bushey Lane Jc.   RAINFORD   PEMBERTON   HINDLEY   ATHERTON   WALKDEN   CLIFTON   VICTORIA
HALL ROAD   MAGHULL   Randle Jc.   BRYN   MOORSIDE   SWINTON   ASHBURYS
BLUNDELLSANDS & CROSBY   OLD ROAN   KIRKBY   GARSWOOD   PATRICROFT   SALFORD
WATERLOO   AINTREE   FAZAKERLEY   NEWTON-LE-WILLOWS   Golborne Jc.   MANCHESTER   BELLE VUE
SEAFORTH   NEW BRIGHTON   ST. HELENS   EARLESTOWN   TRAFFORD PK   LEVENSHULME
WALLASEY GROVE ROAD   THATTO HEATH   East Jc.   IRLAM   FLIXTON   URMSTON
WALLASEY VILLAGE   ECCLESTON PK   Glazebrook Moss Jc.   SALE
MORETON   BIDSTON   PRESCOT   LEA GRN.   ST. HELEN'S JC.   GLAZE   PARTINGTON   BROOKLANDS   STOCKPORT
MEOLS   LIME ST.   ROBY   Winwick   BIRCHWOOD   BROOK   TIMPERLEY   DAVENPORT
MANOR ROAD   CEN.   HUYTON   WHISTON   RAINHILL   Widnes SANKEY   Dam Lane Jc.   HAZEL GROVE
LEASOWE   UPTON   Jc.   WARRINGTON   ALTRINCHAM   CHEADLE HULME
HOYLAKE   BRUNSWICK   HOUGH GREEN   WIDNES   FIDDLERS   LATCHFORD   HALE   HEALD GREEN   STYAL   BRAMHALL
WEST KIRBY   BIRKENHEAD   GARSTON   HALEWOOD   FERRY   Old Main Line Jc.   MANCHESTER AIRPORT   HANDFORTH   POYNTON
   Acton Grange Jc.   MOBBERLEY   WILMSLOW   ADLINGTON
HESWALL   BROMBOROUGH   RUNCORN   TANHOUSE LANE   ASHLEY   KNUTSFORD   ALDERLEY EDGE   Prestbury Tnl.   PRESTBURY
   Halton Jc.   RUNCORN EAST   CHELFORD   Hibel Tnl.
HOOTON   LITTLE SUTTON   STANLOW & THORNTON   Frodsham Jc.   PLUMLEY   MACCLESFIELD
NESTON   OVERPOOL   INCE & ELTON   FRODSHAM   Weaver Jc.   WINNINGTON   LOSTOCK GRALAM
HOLYWELL (TOWN)   ELLESMERE PORT   HELSBY   ACTON BRIDGE   GREENBANK   NORTHWICH   GOOSTREY
CAPENHURST   MOULDS WORTH   CUDDINGTON   HARTFORD   HOLMES CHAPEL
FLINT   North Jc.   DELAMERE   Winsford Jc.
West Jc.   HAWARDEN BRIDGE   BACHE   SANDBACH   CONGLETON   Upper Jc.
East Jc.   East Jc.   CHESTER   WINSFORD
SHOTTON   Mold Jc.   Crewe North Jc.   ALSAGER   KIDSGROVE   Harecastle Tnl.
HAWARDEN   Christleton Tun.   Manchester Line Jc.   CREWE   Basford Hall Jc.   Jamage Jc.
MOLD   BUCKLEY   Tattenhall Jc.   Gresty Lane Jc.   LONGPORT
RUTHIN   PENYFFORDD   NANTWICH   Market Drayton Jc.   ETRURIA
HOPE   CAERGWRLE   WRENBURY   Botteslow Jc.
CEFN-Y-BEDD   STOKE   LONGTON
GWERSYLLT   WREXHAM GENERAL   WHITCHURCH   WEDGWOOD
WREXHAM CENTRAL   BARLASTON
CARROG   DEESIDE HALT   BERWYN   RUABON   STONE
GLYNDYFRDWY   LLANGOLLEN   Berwyn Tun.   PREES   NORTON BRIDGE
Llangollen Railway   CHIRK   MARKET DRAYTON
GLYNCEIRIOG   ELLESMERE   STAFFORD
GOBOWEN   Trent Valley Jc.
Gobowen Jc.   WEM
OSWESTRY   YORTON
Cambrian Railway Society
BLODWELL

1　　　　2　　　Twenty eight　　3　　　4　　　5

REDMIRE

NORTHALLERTON
South Jc.
Cordio Jcs.

Skelton Jc.　Bootham Jc.
Severus Jc.　Burton Lane Jc.
North Jc.　YORK　Foss Islands Jc.
Holgate Bridge

A

Ashton Moss North Jc.　ASHTON-UNDER-LYNE
Crowthorn Jc.　STALYBRIDGE
Audenshaw Jc.
GUIDE BRIDGE
Denton Jc.

MASHAM

THIRSK

HELMSLEY

BARNOLDSWICK
EARBY
COLNE
NELSON

LOFTHOUSE-IN-NIDDERDALE

MELMERBY

RIPON

EASINGWOLD

B

PATELEY BRIDGE

GRASSINGTON & THRESHFIELD

Three Signal Bri. Jc.
Geldard Jc.　LEEDS
Wortley Jc.　Canal Jc. Leeds Jc.
Engine Shed Jc.
Wortley S. Jc.
N. Jc.

RYLSTONE

Bilton Road Jc.
Dragon Jc.
KNARESBRO'　HAMMERTON
STARBECK　CATTAL
HARROGATE
HORNBEAM PARK
Crimple Jc.
Pannal Jc.　Crimple Tun.
PANNAL

YORK
Bootham Jc.
Burton Lane Jc.
POPPLETON
Skelton Jc.
Severus Jc.
Chaloners Whin Jc.　Holgate Bridge Jc.

Twenty four

GARGRAVE
EMBSAY
Skipton N. Jc.　HOLYWELL HALT
SKIPTON
BOLTON ABBEY
Embsay & Bolton Abbey Steam Railway

Wetherby W.Jc.
WETHERBY
Wetherby E.Jc.

Swing Bridge

C

EARBY
CONONLEY
STEETON & SILSDEN
ILKLEY
BEN RHYDDING
BURLEY in WHARFEDALE
Milner Wood Jc.
WEETON

TADCASTER
ULLESKELF
Colton Junction

Inset

OLDHAM
DERKER MUMPS
DAMEMS
WERNETH
Worth Valley Bch.Jc.
West
INGROW WEST
OAKWORTH
HAWORTH
OXENHOPE
Keighley & Worth Valley Railway
KEIGHLEY
CROSSFLATTS
BINGLEY
BAILDON
Bingley Tun.
SALTAIRE　SHIPLEY
FRIZINGHALL
BRADFORD
NEW PUDSEY
Bowling Tun.

YEADON
HORSFORTH
BRAMLEY
COTTINGLEY

LEEDS

Cross Gates Jc.
CROSS GATES
Hunslet Bch Jc.
Stourton Jc.
WOODLES-FORD
LEDSTON

GARFORTH
MICKLEFIELD
EAST GARFORTH
Milford Jc.
SHERBURN-IN-ELMET
SOUTH MILFORD
Gasgoigne Wood Jc.

CHURCH FENTON
CAWOOD
Swing Bri.
E. Jc. Barlby Jc.
SELBY
Brayton N. Jc.
Brayton E. Jc.
WRESSLE

D

MENSTON
GUISELEY
Bramhope Tun.

MORLEY
MORLEY Tun.

Kitson Wood Tun.
Hall Royd Jc.
Millwood Tun.
Weasel Hall Tun.
HEBDEN BRI.
MYTHOLMROYD
Horsfall Tun.
Castle Hill Tun.
TODMORDEN
WALSDEN
Winterbutlee Tun.
Summit Tun.
HALIFAX
Bank House Tun.
SOWERBY BRI.
BRIGHOUSE
Bradley Wood Jc.
MIRFIELD
WYKE Tun.　Wyke Jc.
BATLEY
DEWSBURY
RAVENSTHORPE
L.N.W. Jc.

WAKEFIELD
NORMANTON
CASTLEFORD
PONTEFRACT MONKHILL
KNOTTINGLEY
Temple Hirst Jc.
Gowdall Jc.
WHITLEY BRIDGE
Hensall Jc.　Aire Jc.
HENSALL
DRAX
SNAITH
RAWCLIFFE

STREETHOUSE
TANSHELF
FEATHERSTONE
PONTEFRACT BAGHILL

E

Twenty
RISHWORTH
STAINLAND
Springwood Jc.
DEIGHTON
HUDDERSFIELD
LOCKWOOD
BERRY BROW
Robin Hood Tun.
LITTLEBOROUGH
SMITHY BRIDGE
SLAITHWAITE
HONLEY
STOCKS MOOR
KIRKBURTON
Steeple Grange
Light Railway
CLAYTON WEST
DARTON
Crigglestone Tun.
N. Jc.
S. Jc.
Brackenhill Jc.
W. Jc.
FITZWILLIAM
Royston Jc.
Wrangbrook Jc.
THORNE NORTH
THORNE SOUTH

Rochdale E. Jc.
MILNROW
ROCHDALE
NEW HEY
SHAW & CROMPTON
MARSDEN
Standedge Tun.
MELTHAM
BROCKHOLES
Thurstonland Tun.
SHELLEY
DENBY DALE
CUCKOO'S NEST
SHEPLEY
SKELMANTHORPE
Cumberworth Tun.
Shafton Jc.
MOORTHORPE
Joan Croft Jc.
Applehurst Jc.
Shaftholme Jc.
Thorne Jc.
HATFIELD & STAINFORTH
Adwick Jc.
Skellow Jc.
ADWICK
Castle Hills Jc.
BENTLEY
KIRK SANDALL
Kirk Sandall Jc.
Bentley Jc.

DELPH
Diggle Jc.
GREENFIELD
Royal George Tun.
HOLMFIRTH
Woodhead Tun.
DODWORTH
SILKSTONE COMMON
Wellhouse Jc.
PENISTONE
Barnsley Jc.
BARNSLEY
MONK BRETTON
Ardsley Tun.
THURNSCOE
Hickleton S. Jc.
GOLDTHORPE
BOLTON ON DEARNE
Dearne Jc.
MEXBORO'
ADWICK
DONCASTER
South Yorkshire Jc.
Blackcarr Jc.
Bessacar Jc.
St. Catherine's Jcs.
Loversall Carr Jc.

F

OLDHAM MUMPS
MOSSLEY
Scout Tunnel
ASHTON
STALYBRIDGE
GUIDE BRIDGE
HYDE NORTH
HADFIELD
Denton Jc.
HYDE CENTRAL
DINTING
GLOSSOP
Reddish
WOODLEY
BREDBURY
ROMILEY
WOODHEAD
Woodhead Tun.
BENTLEY
Kirk Sandall Jc.
Bentley Jc.
Marshgate Jc.
DONCASTER
N. Jc.
Bubby Jc.
South Yorkshire Jc.
S.Jc.
Potteric Carr Jc.
Low Ellers Jc.
Hexthorpe
Black Carr Jc.
Doncaster Avoiding Line Jc.
Bessacar Jc.
Loversall Carr Jc.
Black Carr E.Jc.
St. Catherine's Jcs.

WOMBWELL
ELSECAR
SWINTON
WATH Rd. Jc.
CONISBROUGH
STOCKSBRIDGE
CHAPELTOWN
Tankersley Tun.
Braithwell Jc.
Northern Jc.
HARWORTH

G

DAVENPORT
ROSE HILL
HAYFIELD
MARPLE
STRINES
WOODSMOOR
HAZEL GROVE

ROTHERHAM CENTRAL
MEADOWHALL
TINSLEY YARD
Tunnel Jc.
DARNALL
Treeton Jc.
SHEFFIELD
WOODHOUSE
Southern Jc.
DINNINGTON Jc.
(S. YORKS. JC.)

Fifteen　　　　　　　Sixteen

1 Flowery Field
2 Newton for Hyde
3 Godley
4 Hattersley
5 Broadbottom

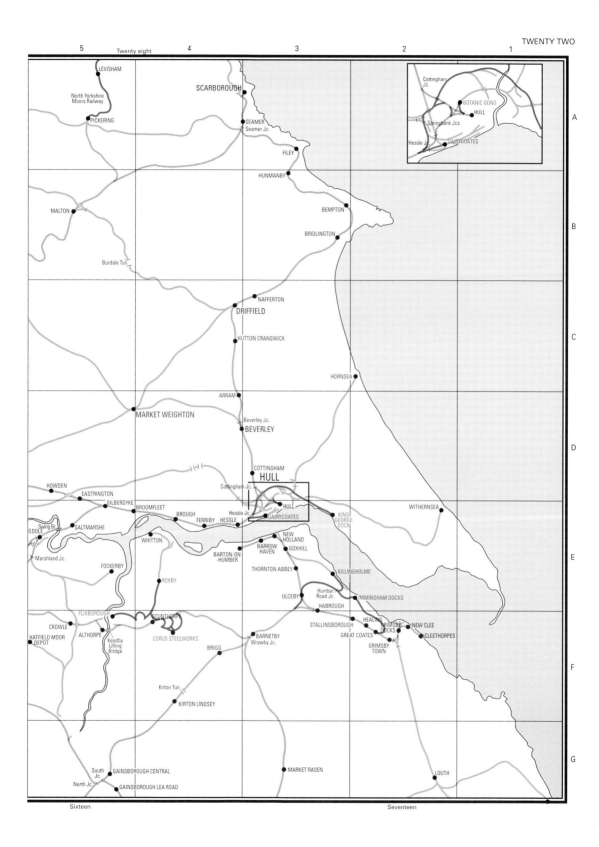

5   Twenty eight   4   3   2   1

Cottingham Jc.
BOTANIC GDNS
HULL
Springbank Jcs
Hessle Jc.
DAIRYCOATES

A

LEVISHAM

North Yorkshire
Moors Railway

PICKERING

SCARBOROUGH

SEAMER
Seamer Jc.

FILEY

HUNMANBY

MALTON

BEMPTON

BRIDLINGTON

B

Burdale Tun.

NAFFERTON

DRIFFIELD

HUTTON CRANSWICK

C

HORNSEA

ARRAM

MARKET WEIGHTON

Beverley Jc.
BEVERLEY

D

HOWDEN

EASTRINGTON

GILBERDYKE

BROOMFLEET

BROUGH

FERRIBY

HESSLE

COTTINGHAM
HULL

Cottingham Jc.

Hessle Jc.
DAIRYCOATES

HULL

KING
GEORGE
DOCK

WITHERNSEA

Swing Br.
GOOLE

SALTMARSHE

WHITTON

NEW
HOLLAND

GOXHILL

E

Marshland Jc.

FOCKERBY

ROXBY

BARTON-ON-
-HUMBER

BARROW
HAVEN

THORNTON ABBEY

KILLINGHOLME

Humber
Road Jc.

IMMINGHAM DOCKS

FLIXBOROUGH

CROWLE

HATFIELD MOOR
DEPOT

ALTHORPE

Keadby
Lifting
Bridge

SCUNTHORPE

CORUS STEELWORKS

BARNETBY
Wrawby Jc.

BRIGG

ULCEBY

HABROUGH

STALLINGBOROUGH

GREAT COATES

HEALING

GRIMSBY
DOCKS

GRIMSBY
TOWN

NEW CLEE

CLEETHORPES

F

Kirton Tun.

KIRTON LINDSEY

South
Jc.

GAINSBOROUGH CENTRAL

North Jc.

GAINSBOROUGH LEA ROAD

MARKET RASEN

LOUTH

G

Sixteen   Seventeen

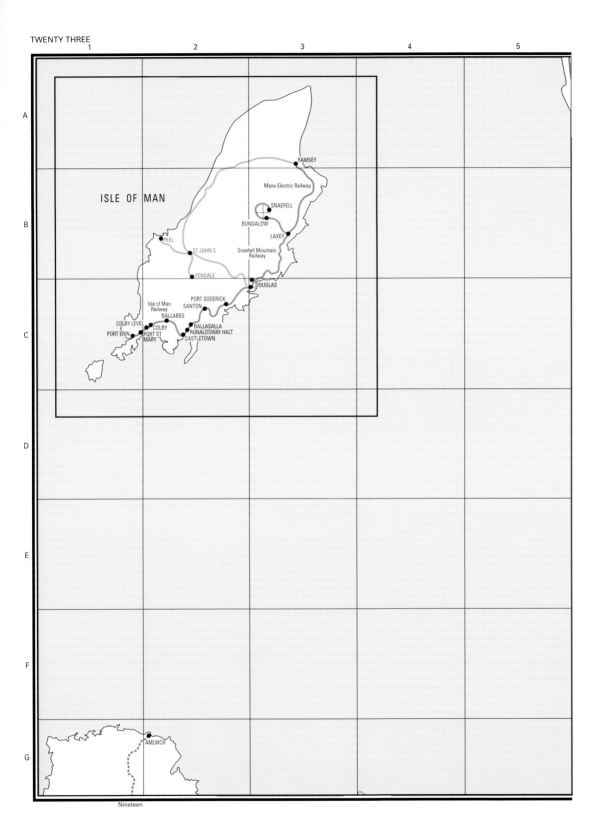

ISLE OF MAN

RAMSEY

Manx Electric Railway

SNAEFELL

BUNGALOW

LAXEY

PEEL

ST JOHN'S

Snaefell Mountain
Railway

FOXDALE

DOUGLAS

PORT SODERICK

SANTON

Isle of Man
Railway

BALLABEG

COLBY LEVEL

COLBY

BALLASALLA

PORT ERIN

PORT ST
MARY

RONALDSWAY HALT

CASTLETOWN

AMLWCH

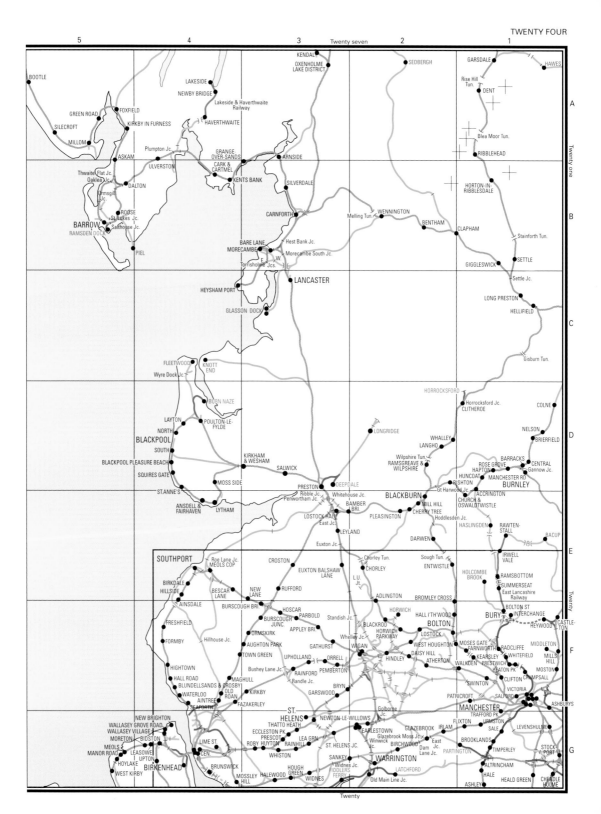

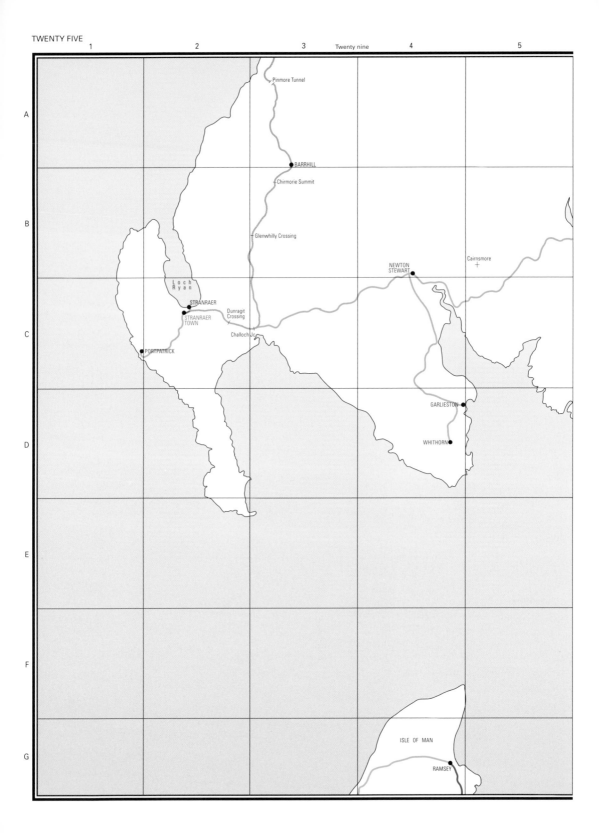

Pinmore Tunnel

●BARRHILL

Chirmorie Summit

Glenwhilly Crossing

Cairnsmore
+

NEWTON
STEWART●

L o c h
R y a n

STRANRAER●

STRANRAER
TOWN

Dunragit
Crossing

Challoch Jc.

●PORTPATRICK

GARLIESTON●

WHITHORN●

ISLE OF MAN

RAMSEY●

Twenty nine

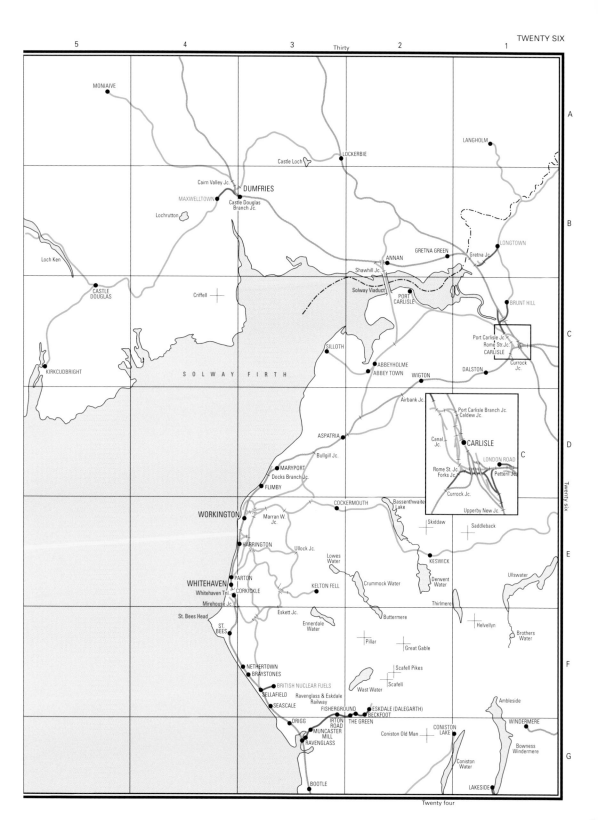

5   4   3   Thirty   2   1

A

MONIAIVE

LANGHOLM

Castle Loch

LOCKERBIE

Cairn Valley Jc.

DUMFRIES

MAXWELLTOWN

Castle Douglas
Branch Jc.

Lochrutton

B

LONGTOWN

GRETNA GREEN

ANNAN

Gretna Jc.

Shawhill Jc.

Loch Ken

Solway Viaduct

PORT
CARLISLE

BRUNT HILL

CASTLE
DOUGLAS

Criffell

Port Carlisle Jc.

Rome Str.Jc.

CARLISLE

C

SILLOTH

Currock
Jc.

KIRKCUDBRIGHT

S O L W A Y   F I R T H

ABBEYHOLME

ABBEY TOWN

WIGTON

DALSTON

Airbank Jc.

Port Carlisle Branch Jc.
Caldew Jc.

ASPATRIA

Canal
Jc.

CARLISLE

D

Bullgill Jc.

LONDON ROAD

C

MARYPORT

Rome St. Jc.

Docks Branch Jc.

Forks Jc.

Petteril Jc.

FLIMBY

COCKERMOUTH

Bassenthwaite
Lake

Currock Jc.

WORKINGTON

Marran W.
Jc.

Skiddaw

Saddleback

Upperby New Jc.

Twenty six

HARRINGTON

Ullock Jc.

KESWICK

Ullswater

E

Lowes
Water

PARTON

Derwent
Water

WHITEHAVEN

CORKICKLE

KELTON FELL

Crummock Water

Whitehaven Tnl.

Thirlmere

Mirehouse Jc.

Eskett Jc.

St. Bees Head

Ennerdale
Water

Buttermere

Helvellyn

ST.
BEES

Pillar

Great Gable

Brothers
Water

F

NETHERTOWN

Scafell Pikes

BRAYSTONES

Scafell

Ambleside

BRITISH NUCLEAR FUELS

Wast Water

SELLAFIELD

Ravenglass & Eskdale
Railway

WINDERMERE

SEASCALE

FISHERGROUND

ESKDALE (DALEGARTH)
BECKFOOT

DRIGG

IRTON
ROAD

THE GREEN

CONISTON
LAKE

Bowness
Windermere

MUNCASTER
MILL

Coniston Old Man

RAVENGLASS

Coniston
Water

G

BOOTLE

LAKESIDE

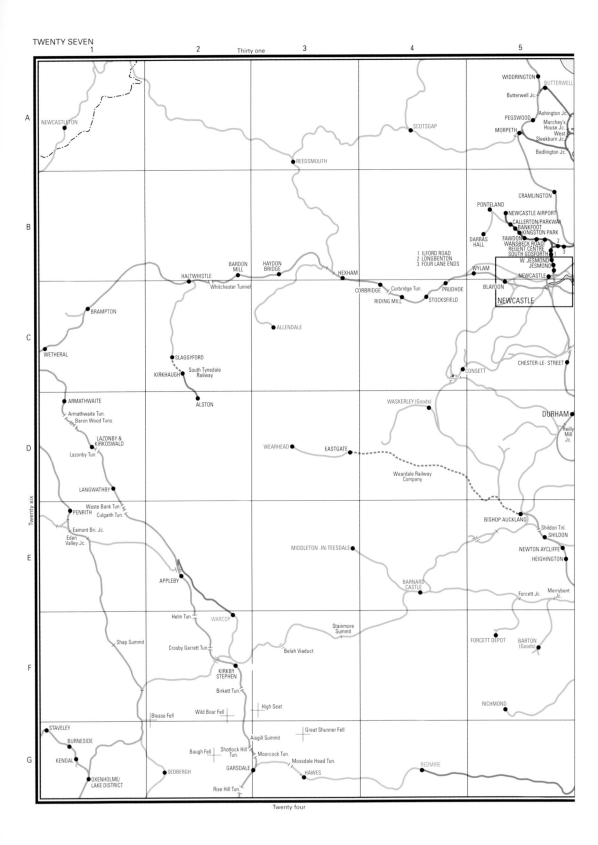

A

B

C

D

E

F

G

Twenty six

WIDDRINGTON
BUTTERWELL
Butterwell Jc.
PEGSWOOD
Ashington Jc.
Marchey's House Jc.
West Sleekburn Jc.
MORPETH
Bedlington Jc.

CRAMLINGTON
PONTELAND
NEWCASTLE AIRPORT
CALLERTON/PARKWAY
BANKFOOT
KINGSTON PARK
DARRAS HALL
FAWDON
KINGSTON
WANSBECK ROAD
REGENT CENTRE
SOUTH GOSFORTH
1 ILFORD ROAD
2 LONGBENTON
3 FOUR LANE ENDS
W. JESMOND
JESMOND
NEWCASTLE
WYLAM
BLAYDON
NEWCASTLE

NEWCASTLETON

SCOTSGAP

REEDSMOUTH

BARDON MILL
HAYDON BRIDGE
HALTWHISTLE
Whitchester Tunnel
HEXHAM
CORBRIDGE
Corbridge Tun.
PRUDHOE
RIDING MILL
STOCKSFIELD

BRAMPTON

ALLENDALE

CONSETT

CHESTER-LE-STREET

WETHERAL
SLAGGYFORD
KIRKHAUGH
South Tynedale Railway

ARMATHWAITE
Armathwaite Tun.
Baron Wood Tuns.
ALSTON

WASKERLEY (Goods)

DURHAM
Reilly Mill Jc.

LAZONBY & KIRKOSWALD
Lazonby Tun.

WEARHEAD
EASTGATE
Weardale Railway Company

LANGWATHBY

PENRITH
Waste Bank Tun.
Culgaith Tun.
Eamont Bri. Jc.
Eden Valley Jc.

BISHOP AUCKLAND
Shildon Tnl.
SHILDON
NEWTON AYCLIFFE
HEIGHINGTON

MIDDLETON-IN-TEESDALE

APPLEBY

BARNARD CASTLE
Forcett Jc.
Merrybent Jc.

Helm Tun.
WARCOP
Stainmore Summit

Shap Summit
Crosby Garrett Tun.
Belah Viaduct

FORCETT DEPOT
BARTON (Goods)

KIRKBY STEPHEN
Birkett Tun.

RICHMOND

High Seat

Blease Fell
Wild Boar Fell

STAVELEY
Great Shunner Fell

BURNESIDE
Aisgill Summit

KENDAL
Baugh Fell
Shotlock Hill Tun.
Moorcock Tun.
Mossdale Head Tun.

OXENHOLME/LAKE DISTRICT
SEDBERGH
GARSDALE
HAWES
Rise Hill Tun.
REDMIRE

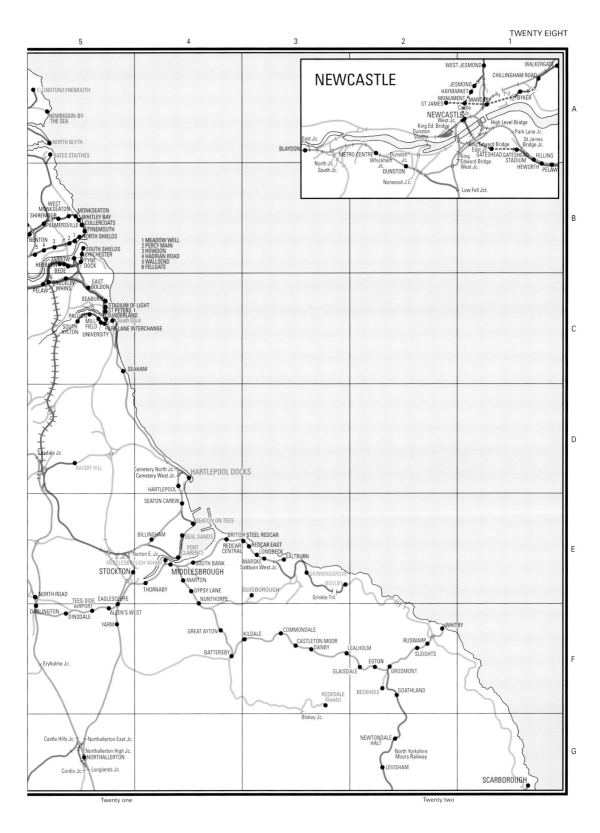

5   4   3   2   1

NEWCASTLE

WEST JESMOND
WALKERGATE
CHILLINGHAM ROAD
JESMOND
HAYMARKET
MONUMENT MANORS
ST JAMES Castle
NEWCASTLE BYKER
West Jc.
King Ed. Bridge High Level Bridge
Dunston Park Lane Jc.
East Jc. Staiths St James
BLAYDON King Edward Bridge Bridge Jc.
METRO CENTRE Dunston GATESHEAD FELLING
Whickham Jc. King GATESHEAD
North Jc. Jc. Edward Bridge STADIUM
South Jc. DUNSTON West Jc. HEWORTH
Norwood J.c. PELAW
Low Fell Jct.

ELLINGTON/LYNEMOUTH

NEWBIGGIN-BY-
THE SEA

NORTH BLYTH
BATES STAITHES

WEST
MONKSEATON MONKSEATON
SHIREMOOR WHITLEY BAY
PALMERSVILLE CULLERCOATS
TYNEMOUTH
BENTON NORTH SHIELDS
5 4 3 2 1
SOUTH SHIELDS
JARROW CHICHESTER
HEBBURN TYNE
BEDE DOCK
6
PELAW BROCKLEY EAST
WHINS BOLDON
SEABURN
STADIUM OF LIGHT
ST PETERS
SUNDERLAND
PALLION South Dock
MILL PARK LANE INTERCHANGE
SOUTH FIELD
HYLTON UNIVERSITY

1 MEADOW WELL
2 PERCY MAIN
3 HOWDON
4 HADRIAN ROAD
5 WALLSEND
6 FELLGATE

SEAHAM

Tursdale Jc.

RAISBY HILL

Cemetery North Jc. HARTLEPOOL DOCKS
Cemetery West Jc.

HARTLEPOOL

SEATON CAREW

SEATON ON TEES
SEAL SANDS BRITISH STEEL REDCAR
BILLINGHAM PORT REDCAR EAST
CLARENCE REDCAR LONGBECK
S. Jc. Norton E. Jc. CENTRAL SALTBURN
MIDDLESBROUGH WHARF SOUTH BANK MARSKE
STOCKTON MIDDLESBROUGH Saltburn West Jc.
MARTON SKINNINGGROVE
THORNABY GYPSY LANE GUISBOROUGH BOULBY
NORTH ROAD NUNTHORPE Grinkle Tnl.
TEES-SIDE EAGLESCLIFFE
DARLINGTON AIRPORT ALLEN'S WEST
DINSDALE WHITBY
YARM GREAT AYTON COMMONDALE RUSWARP
KILDALE CASTLETON MOOR SLEIGHTS
Eryholme Jc. BATTERSBY DANBY LEALHOLM
EGTON GROSMONT
GLAISDALE GROSMONT
GLAISDALE GOATHLAND
ROSEDALE BECKHOLE
(Goods)
Blakey Jc.

Castle Hills Jc. Northallerton East Jc. NEWTONDALE
Northallerton High Jc. HALT
NORTHALLERTON North Yorkshire
Cordio Jc. Longlands Jc. Moors Railway
LEVISHAM
SCARBOROUGH

1　　　2　　　3　　　4　　　5

A

B

C

D

E

F

G

Ben Lomond

Loch Long
Summit
Loch Goil

Loch Lomond

ABERFOYLE

GARELOCHHEAD

Gore Loch

GARTNESS

Campsie Fells

HELENSBURGH
(UPPER)
BALLOCH

HELENSBURGH
CENTRAL
CRAIGENDORAN

LENNOXTOWN

ALEXANDRIA

GOUROCK

CARDROSS
RENTON

GREENOCK
CENTRAL
DALREOCH
DUMBARTON CENTRAL
DUMBARTON EAST

MILNGAVIE

KIRKINTILLOCH
Waterside
Jc.

FORT MATILDA
CARTSDYKE
GREENOCK W.
BOGSTON
WOODHALL
BOWLING
KILPATRICK
HILLFOOT
LENZIE
Campsie
Bch. Jc.
Bridgend
Jc.

IBM
BRANCHTON
WHINHILL
PORT
GLASGOW
DALMUIR
BEARSDEN
Milngavie Jc.
MARYHILL
BISHOPBRIGGS
SPRINGBURN

DRUMFROCHAR
LANGBANK
SINGER
YOKER
STEPPS

INVERKIP
Inverkip Tnl.
Bishopton No 2 Tnl.
BISHOPTON

QUEEN ST
CENTRAL
BLAIRHILL

WEMYSS BAY
Blackstone Jc.
GARROWHILL

CARNTYNE
SHETTLESTON

FIRTH OF
CLYDE
Hill of Stake
PAISLEY CROOKSTON
CANAL
CROSSMYLOOF
RUTHERGLEN
CARMYLE

BUTE
JOHNSTONE
NITSHILL
CATHCART
UDDINGSTON

MILLIKEN
PARK
BARRHEAD
THORNLIEBANK
GIFFNOCK
CAMBUSLANG
BURNSIDE
NEWTON

LARGS
HOWWOOD
NEILSTON
MUIREND
CLARKSTON
KIRKHILL
BLANTYRE

LOCHWINNOCH
PATTERTON
WHITE-
CRAIGS
BUSBY

Pier
East Jc.
SEE SHEET NO:
FORTY FOUR
THORNTONHALL

Fairlie Tnl.
FAIRLIE
GLENGARNOCK
HAIRMYRES
EAST
KILBRIDE

GIFFEN
DUNLOP
L
A

WEST KILBRIDE
DALRY
Dalry Jc.
STRATHAVEN NTH.
CEN.

STEWARTON
RYELAND

SALTCOATS
TOWN
KILWINNING

ARDROSSAN
HARBOUR
Dubbs
Jc.
KILMAURS
Kaypark Jc.
County Boundary Jc.

SOUTH BEACH
STEVENSTON
IRVINE
KILMARNOCK

ARRAN
Bellfield Jc.

BARASSIE
MUIRKIRK

TROON
Mossgeil Tnl.

Lochgreen Jc.
Mossblown Jc.
Mauchline Jc.
CATRINE

PRESTWICK INTERNATIONAL AIRPORT
PRESTWICK TOWN
Brackenhill Jc.
CRONBERRY

Falkland Jc.
NEWTON-ON-AYR
AUCHINLECK
Logan Jc.

Blackhouse Jc.
Hawkhill Jc.
KILLOCH

AYR
Belston Jc.

HEADS OF AYR
Alloway Jc.
Dalrymple Jc.
NEW CUMNOCK

BROOMHILL

MAYBOLE
WATERSIDE
Blackcraig Hill

CHALMERSTON

Ayrshire Railway
Preservation Society
DALMELLINGTON

KINTYRE

CAMPBELTOWN

MACHRIHANISH

CAMPBELTOWN & MACHRIHANISH
LIGHT RAILWAY

GIRVAN
Tunnel

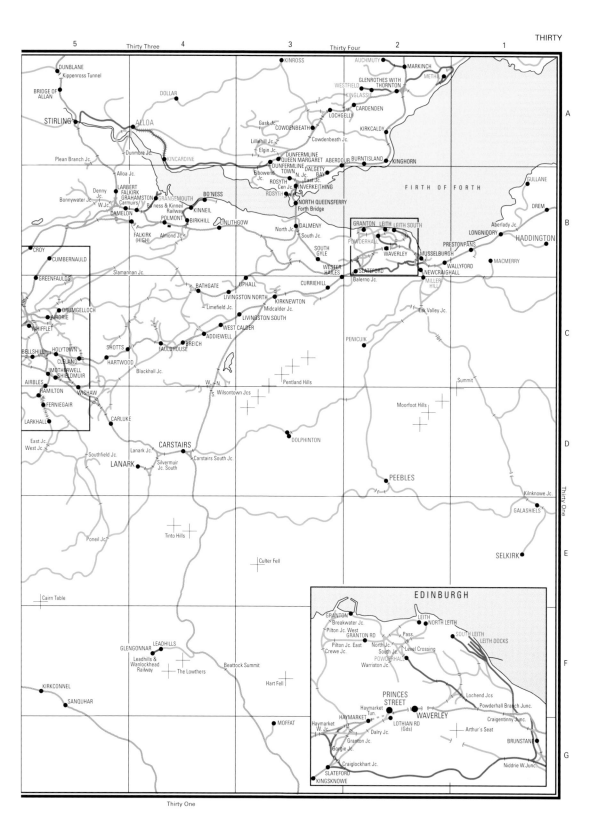

DUNBLANE
Kippenross Tunnel
BRIDGE OF
ALLAN
STIRLING
DOLLAR
ALLOA
KINCARDINE
Plean Branch Jc.
Dunmore Jc.
KINROSS
AUCHMUTY   MARKINCH
METHIL
GLENROTHES WITH
THORNTON
WESTFIELD
KINGLASSIE
LOCHGELLY
CARDENDEN
Gask Jc.   COWDENBEATH
Lilliehill Jc.   Cowdenbeath Jc.   KIRKCALDY
Elgin Jc.
DUNFERMLINE
QUEEN MARGARET   ABERDOUR   BURNTISLAND
DUNFERMLINE   DALGETY
Elbowend   TOWN   N. Jc.   BAY   KINGHORN
Jc.   East Jc.
ROSYTH   Cen Jc.   INVERKEITHING
ROSYTH   FIRTH OF FORTH
NORTH QUEENSFERRY
Forth Bridge

Denny   LARBERT
Jc.   FALKIRK
Bonnywater Jc.   GRAHAMSTON   BO'NESS
W.Jc.   Carmuirs/   Bo'ness & Kinneil
CAMELON   Railway
KINNEIL
GRANGEMOUTH
POLMONT
FALKIRK   BIRKHILL   LINLITHGOW
(HIGH)   Almond Jc.
North Jc.   DALMENY
South Jc.

Alloa Jc.   GULLANE
DREM
Aberlady Jc.   LONGNIDDRY
HADDINGTON
PRESTONPANS
WALLYFORD
NEWCRAIGHALL
MACMERRY

GRANTON   LEITH   LEITH SOUTH
POWDERHALL
WAVERLEY   MUSSELBURGH
SLATEFORD
Balerno Jc.   MILLER
HILL

CROY
CUMBERNAULD
GREENFAULDS
Slamannan Jc.

SOUTH
GYLE
WESTER
HAILES
BATHGATE   UPHALL
LIVINGSTON NORTH
KIRKNEWTON
CURRIEHILL
Limefield Jc.   Midcalder Jc.
LIVINGSTON SOUTH
WEST CALDER
ADDIEWELL
BREICH
SHOTTS   FAULDHOUSE
HARTWOOD
Blackhall Jc.

DRUMGELLOCH
AIRDRIE
WHIFFLET
BELLSHILL   HOLYTOWN
CLELAND
MOTHERWELL
AIRBLES   SHIELDMUIR
HAMILTON   WISHAW
FERNIEGAIR
LARKHALL
CARLUKE

PENICUIK

Esk Valley Jc.

W. — N.
S. Wilsontown Jcs
Pentland Hills
Summit

Moorfoot Hills

East Jc.
West Jc.
Southfield Jc.   Lanark Jc.   CARSTAIRS
Silvermuir   Carstairs South Jc.
Jc. South
LANARK

DOLPHINTON

PEEBLES

Kilknowe Jc.
GALASHIELS

Poneil Jc.
Tinto Hills

SELKIRK

Cairn Table

Culter Fell

GLENGONNAR   LEADHILLS
Leadhills &
Wanlockhead   Beattock Summit
Railway   The Lowthers
Hart Fell
MOFFAT

KIRKCONNEL
SANQUHAR

EDINBURGH

GRANTON
Breakwater Jc.   LEITH
Pilton Jc. West   NORTH LEITH
GRANTON RD
Pilton Jc. East   Pass
Crewe Jc.   North Jc.   Level Crossing   SOUTH LEITH
South Jc.   LEITH DOCKS
POWDERHALL
Warriston Jc.

PRINCES
STREET   Lochend Jcs
WAVERLEY
Haymarket   POWDERHALL Branch Junc.
HAYMARKET   Tun.
Haymarket   LOTHIAN RD   Craigentinny Junc.
W.Jc.   Dalry Jc.   (Gds)
Granton Jc.   Arthur's Seat   BRUNSTANE
Gorgie Jc.
Craiglockhart Jc.   Niddrie W.Junc.
SLATEFORD
KINGSKNOWE

A

B

C

D

E

F

G

Thirty One

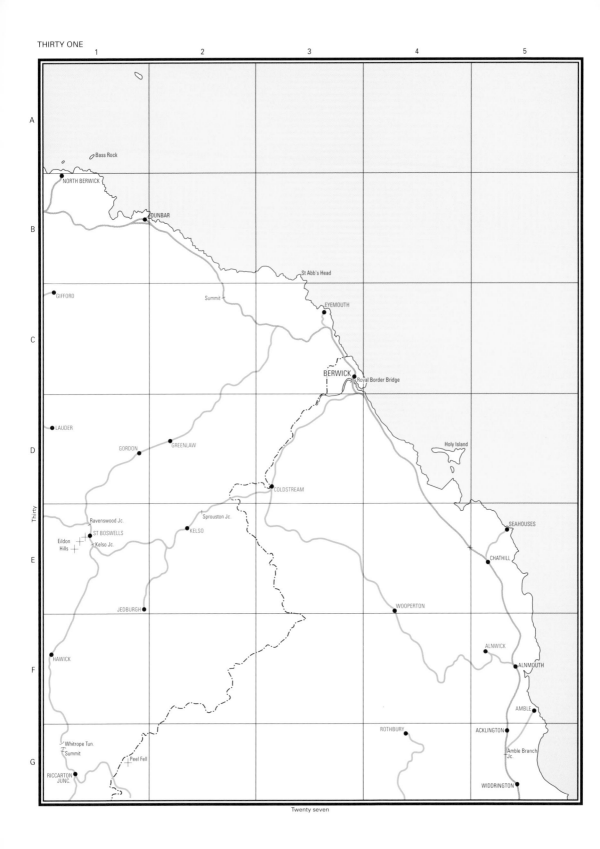

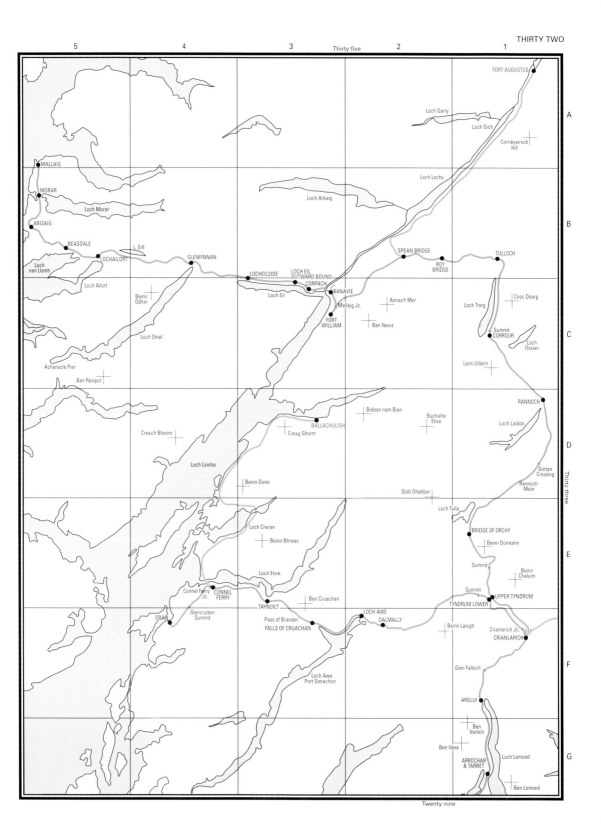

FORT AUGUSTUS

Loch Garry

Loch Oich

A

Corrieyairock
Hill

MALLAIG

MORAR

Loch Lochy

Loch Morar

ARISAIG

B

BEASDALE

Loch Arkaig

L. Eilt

SPEAN BRIDGE

TULLOCH

Loch
nan Uamh

LOCHAILORT

GLENFINNAN

ROY
BRIDGE

Loch Ailort

LOCHEILSIDE

LOCH EIL
OUTWARD BOUND

Beinn
Odhar

Loch Eil

CORPACH

BANAVIE

Cnoc Dearg

Aonach Mor

Loch Treig

Mallaig Jc.

Loch Shiel

FORT
WILLIAM

Ben Nevis

Summit
CORROUR

C

Loch
Ossian

Acharacle Pier

Leim Uilleim

Ben Resipol

Bidean nam Bian

RANNOCH

Buchaille
Etive

BALLACHULISH

Creach Bheinn

Loch Laidon

Creag Ghorm

D

Loch Linnhe

Gortan
Crossing

Beinn Donn

Rannoch
Moor

Stob Ghabbar

Loch Tulla

Loch Creran

BRIDGE OF ORCHY

Beinn Bhreac

Beinn Doireann

E

Summit

Beinn
Chaluim

Loch Etive

Summit

Connel Ferry
Jc.

CONNEL
FERRY

Summit

UPPER TYNDRUM

Ben Cruachan

TAYNUILT

TYNDRUM LOWER

OBAN

Glencruiten
Summit

LOCH AWE

Pass of Brander
FALLS OF CRUACHAN

DALMALLY

Crianlarich Jc.

Beinn Laoigh

CRIANLARICH

F

Glen Falloch

Loch Awe
Port Sonachon

ARDLUI

Ben
Vorlich

Ben Vane

G

ARROCHAR
& TARBET

Loch Lomond

Ben Lomond

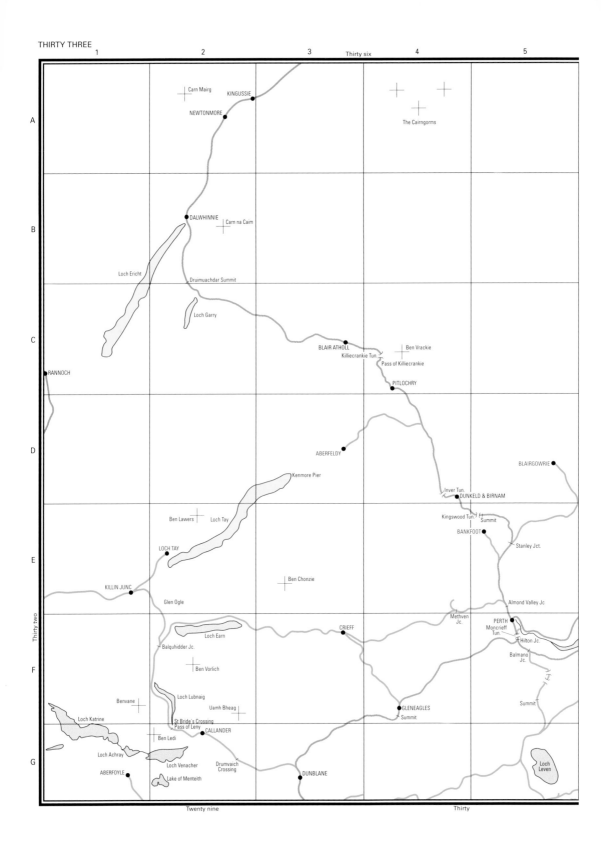

1   2   3   4   5

A

Carn Mairg

KINGUSSIE

NEWTONMORE

The Cairngorms

B

DALWHINNIE

Carn na Caim

Loch Ericht

Druimuachdar Summit

Loch Garry

C

BLAIR ATHOLL

Killiecrankie Tun.

Ben Vrackie

Pass of Killiecrankie

RANNOCH

PITLOCHRY

D

ABERFELDY

BLAIRGOWRIE

Kenmore Pier

Inver Tun.

DUNKELD & BIRNAM

Ben Lawers

Loch Tay

Kingswood Tun.

Summit

LOCH TAY

BANKFOOT

Stanley Jct.

E

KILLIN JUNC

Ben Chonzie

Almond Valley Jc

Glen Ogle

Methven

Jc.

PERTH

CRIEFF

Moncrieff

Tun.

Loch Earn

Hilton Jc.

Balquhidder Jc.

Balmano

Jc.

Ben Vorlich

F

Loch Lubnaig

Benvane

Summit

Uamh Bheag

Loch Katrine

St Bride's Crossing

GLENEAGLES

Pass of Leny

CALLANDER

Summit

Ben Ledi

Loch Achray

Loch Venacher

Drumvaich

Crossing

Loch

Leven

G

ABERFOYLE

Lake of Menteith

DUNBLANE

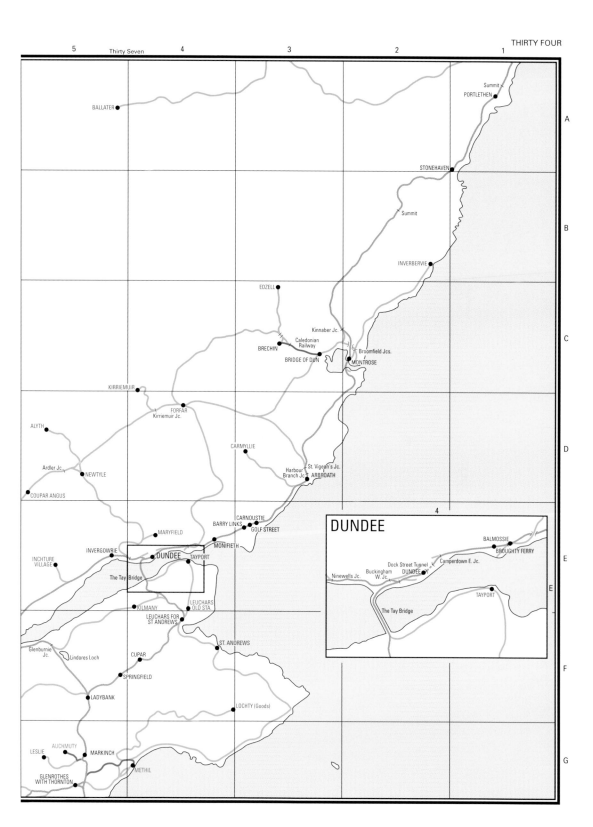

A

B

C

D

E

F

G

BALLATER

Summit
PORTLETHEN

STONEHAVEN

Summit

INVERBERVIE

EDZELL

Kinnaber Jc.

Caledonian
Railway

BRECHIN

BRIDGE OF DUN

Broomfield Jcs.
MONTROSE

KIRRIEMUIR

FORFAR
Kirriemuir Jc.

ALYTH

Ardler Jc.
NEWTYLE

COUPAR ANGUS

CARMYLLIE

St. Vigean's Jc.
Harbour
Branch Jc. ARBROATH

CARNOUSTIE
BARRY LINKS
GOLF STREET
MONIFIETH

MARYFIELD

INVERGOWRIE
DUNDEE   TAYPORT

INCHTURE
VILLAGE

The Tay Bridge

KILMANY

LEUCHARS
OLD STA.

LEUCHARS FOR
ST ANDREWS

Glenburnie
Jc. Lindores Loch

CUPAR

ST. ANDREWS

SPRINGFIELD

LADYBANK

LOCHTY (Goods)

LESLIE   AUCHMUTY

MARKINCH

GLENROTHES
WITH THORNTON

METHIL

DUNDEE

4

BALMOSSIE
BROUGHTY FERRY

Dock Street Tunnel
Buckingham   Camperdown E. Jc.
Ninewells Jc.   W. Jc.   DUNDEE

TAYPORT

The Tay Bridge

E

E

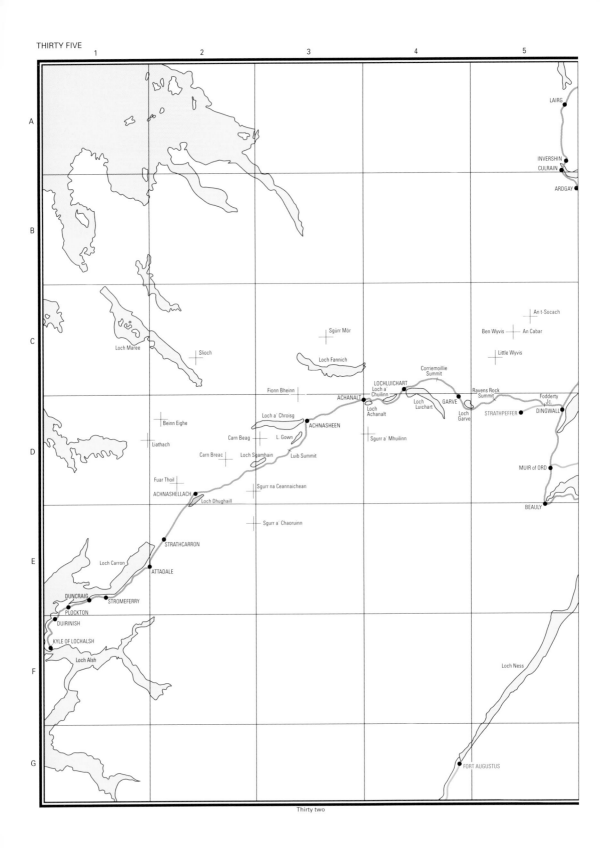

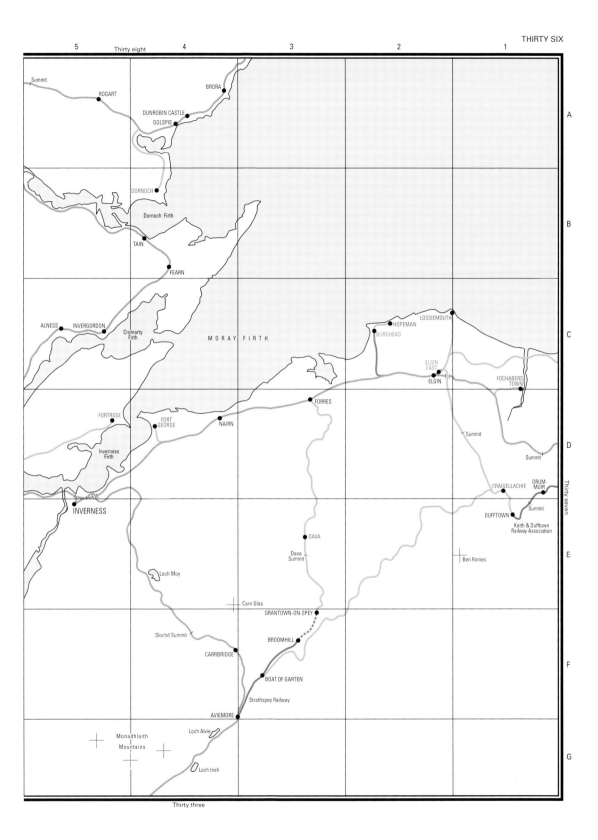

Summit
ROGART
BRORA
DUNROBIN CASTLE
GOLSPIE

A

DORNOCH

Dornoch Firth

B

TAIN

FEARN

LOSSIEMOUTH
HOPEMAN
ALNESS   INVERGORDON   BURGHEAD
Cromarty
Firth   M O R A Y   F I R E T H

ELGIN
EAST
ELGIN   FOCHABERS
TOWN

C

FORTROSE   FORRES
FORT
GEORGE   NAIRN   Summit

Inverness
Firth   Summit

D

CRAIGELLACHIE   DRUM-
MUIR
Thirty seven
INVERNESS   Summit
DUFFTOWN
Keith & Dufftown
Railway Association

Loch Moy   DAVA

Dava
Summit   Ben Rinnes

E

Carn Glas
GRANTOWN-ON-SPEY
Slochd Summit   BROOMHILL
CARRBRIDGE

F

BOAT OF GARTEN
Strathspey Railway
AVIEMORE

Loch Alvie
Monadhlaith
Mountains

Loch Insh

G

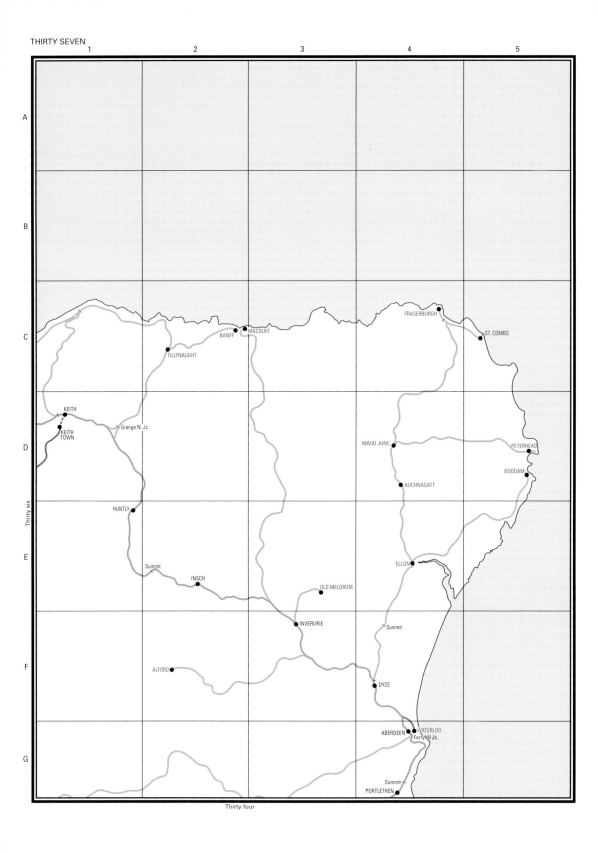

A

B

C

FRASERBURGH

ST. COMBS

BANFF MACDUFF

TILLYNAUGHT

KEITH

Grange N. Jc.

KEITH TOWN

MAUD JUNC.

PETERHEAD

BODDAM

AUCHNAGATT

Thirty six

HUNTLY

E

ELLON

Summit

INSCH

OLD MELDRUM

INVERURIE

Summit

F

ALFORD

DYCE

WATERLOO

ABERDEEN
Ferryhill Jc.

G

Summit

PORTLETHEN

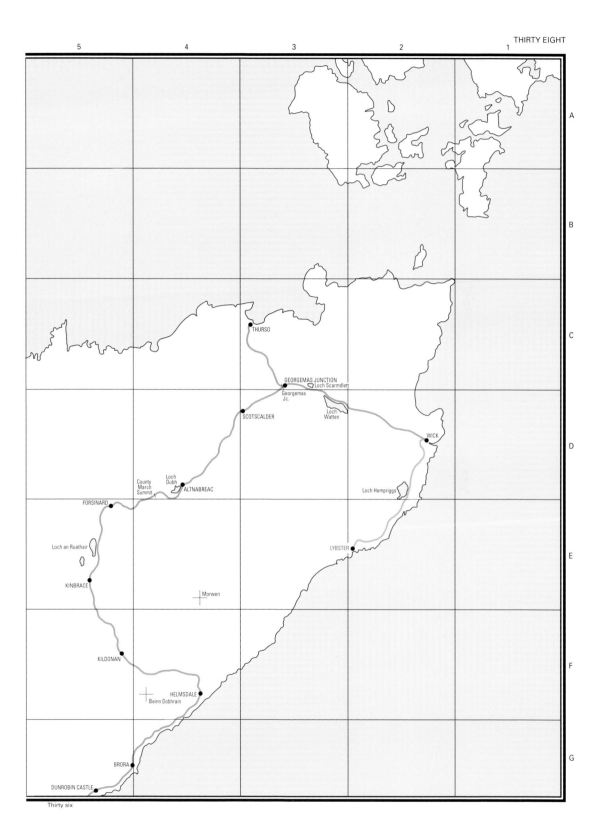

5   4   3   2   1

A

B

THURSO

GEORGEMAS JUNCTION
Loch Scarmdlett
Georgemas
Jc.
SCOTSCALDER
Loch
Watten
WICK

C

Loch
Dubh   ALTNABREAC
County
March
Summit
FORSINARD
Loch Hempriggs

D

Loch an Ruathair
LYBSTER

E

KINBRACE
Morwen

KILDONAN
HELMSDALE
Beinn Dobhrain

F

BRORA
DUNROBIN CASTLE

G

1   2   3   4   5

A

PINNER
HARROW & WEALDSTONE
NORTH HARROW
HARROW-ON-THE-HILL
KENTON
NORTHWICK PARK
WEST HARROW
North Jc. South Jc.
SOUTH KENTON
QUEENSBURY
COLINDALE
KINGSBURY
PRESTON ROAD
HENDON CENTRAL
HENDON
BRENT CROSS
EAST FINCHLEY
HIGHGATE WOOD SIDINGS HIGHGATE
NORTHERN LINE TO CENTRAL LONDON
GOLDERS GREEN

B

EASTCOTE
RAYNERS LANE
SOUTH HARROW
NORTHOLT PARK
NORTH WEMBLEY
SUDBURY HILL HARROW
SUDBURY & HARROW RD.
WEMBLEY PARK
SOUTH RUISLIP
NORTHOLT
GREENFORD
SUDBURY HILL
SUDBURY TOWN
WEMBLEY STADIUM
WEMBLEY CENTRAL
STONEBRIDGE PARK
NEASDEN
Neasden S. Jc.
Neasden Jc.
DOLLIS HILL KILBURN
WILLESDEN GREEN
BRONDESBURY
Dudding Jc.
CRICKLEWOOD
WEST HAMPSTEAD THAMESLINK
WEST HAMPSTEAD & FROGNAL
FINCHLEY RD
HAMPSTEAD HEATH
GOSPEL OAK
Haverstock Hill Tun.
Carlton Rd Jc.
SWISS COTTAGE
Canfield Place
SOUTH HAMPSTEAD
KILBURN
Primrose Hill Tuns.
St John's WoodTun
ST JOHN'S WOOD
NORTHERN LINE TO CENTRAL LONDON
ALPERTON
HARLESDEN
KENSAL RISE
BRONDESBURY PARK
QUEEN'S PARK
Kensal Green Jc.
KENSAL GREEN
Kensal Green Tuns
Lords Tun.
GREAT PORTLAND ST
BAKER STREET

C

SOUTH GREENFORD
PERIVALE
Brent Jc.
WILLESDEN JUNC.
West London Jc.
N. & S.W.
Old Oak Jc.
Mitre Bri. Jc.
MITRE BRIDGE
Portobello
NORTH POLE DEPOT
ROYAL OAK
WESTBOURNE PARK
LADBROKE GROVE
MARYLEBONE
EDGWARE RD
PADDINGTON
WESTBOURNE PARK
Portobello Jc.
Green Lane Jc.
Level Crossing
PADDINGTON (H&C)
MILEAGE YARD Goods & Coal
PADDINGTON
CASTLE BAR PARK
HANGER LANE
PARK ROYAL
NORTH EALING
Acton Wells Jc.
Old Oak Common W. Jc.
North Pole Jc.
NORTH KENSINGTON
BAYSWATER
LATIMER ROAD
DRAYTON GREEN
EALING BROADWAY
WEST ACTON
NORTH ACTON
EAST ACTON
WHITE CITY
SHEPHERDS BUSH
NOTTING HILL GATE
HANWELL
WEST EALING
EALING COMMON
ACTON MAINLINE
ACTON CENTRAL
Uxbridge Rd Jc.
SHEPHERD'S BUSH
CENTRAL LONDON
HIGH ST KENSINGTON
VICTORIA
SOUTHALL
Hanwell Jc.
Drayton Green Jc.

D

N. Jc.
ACTON TOWN
N. Jc.
Acton Jc.
CITY ACTON
TURNHAM GREEN
GOLDHAWK RD.
OLYMPIA
Cromwell Curve North Jc.
GLOUCESTER RD
SLOANE SQUARE
SOUTH EALING
NORTHFIELDS
Bollo Lane Jc.
Brentford Lane Jc.
Acton Lane Jc.
Studland Rd Jc.
STAMFORD BROOK
RAVENSCOURT PARK
HAMMERSMITH
BARON'S COURT
WEST KENSINGTON
EARLS COURT
Cromwell Curve South Jc.
STH. KENSINGTON
GUNNERSBURY
HAMMERSMITH & CHISWICK
BOSTON MANOR
BRENTFORD
Old Jc.
KEW BRIDGE
East Jc.
New Jc.
CHISWICK
BARNES BRIDGE
WEST BROMPTON
FULHAM BROADWAY
Chelsea Basin Jc.
Battersea Wharf
BATTERSEA PARK
QUEENSTOWN ROAD
OSTERLEY
HOUNSLOW EAST
SYON LANE
ISLEWORTH
BRENTFORD GOODS
KEW GARDENS
BARNES
PARSONS GREEN
PUTNEY BRI.
HOUNSLOW WEST
HOUNSLOW CENTRAL
HOUNSLOW
RICHMOND
NORTH SHEEN
MORTLAKE
PUTNEY
WANDSWORTH TOWN
Latchmere Jcs
CLAPHAM JUNCTION

E

Hounslow Jc.
Feltham Jc.
WHITTON
Whitton Jc.
TWICKENHAM
ST. MARGARETS
Latchmere S.W. Jc.
Battersea Pier Jc.
Battersea Wharf
EAST PUTNEY
Point Pleasant Jc.
WANDSWORTH COMMON
BALHAM
STRAWBERRY HILL
Strawberry Hill Jc.
Fulwell Jc.
FULWELL
Shacklegate Jc.
CLAPHAM JUNCTION
Ludgate Jc.
Latchmere Main Jc.
Longhedge Jc.
Poupart's Jc.
QUEEN'S RD
BATTERSEA PARK
Stewarts Lane Jc.
SOUTHFIELDS
EARLSFIELD
Balham Jc.
WIMBLEDON PARK
NORTHERN LINE TO CENTRAL LONDON
TOOTING BEC

F

HAMPTON
TEDDINGTON
KINGSTON
NORBITON
HAMPTON WICK
NEW MALDEN
Falcon Jc.
Coal Yard Jc.
FALCON LANE
STEWARTS LANE
Factory Jc.
WIMBLEDON
DUNDONALD ROAD
RAYNES PARK
WIMBLEDON CHASE
MERTON PARK
HAYDONS RD
SOUTH WIMBLEDON
COLLIERS WOOD
TOOTING BROADWAY
TOOTING
MORDEN ROAD

G

HAMPTON COURT
THAMES DITTON
SURBITON
Hampton Court Jc.
BERRYLANDS
MALDEN MANOR
WORCESTER PARK
MOTSPUR PARK
SOUTH MERTON
MORDEN SOUTH
ST HELIER
PHIPPS BRIDGE
MORDEN
BELGRAVE WALK
MITCHAM
MITCHAM JUNC.
ESHER
TOLWORTH
SUTTON COMMON
HACKBRIDGE

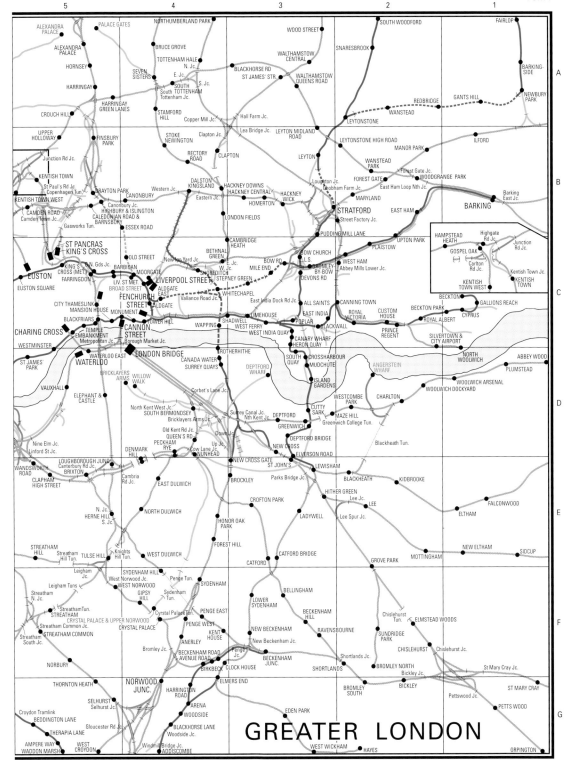

GREATER LONDON

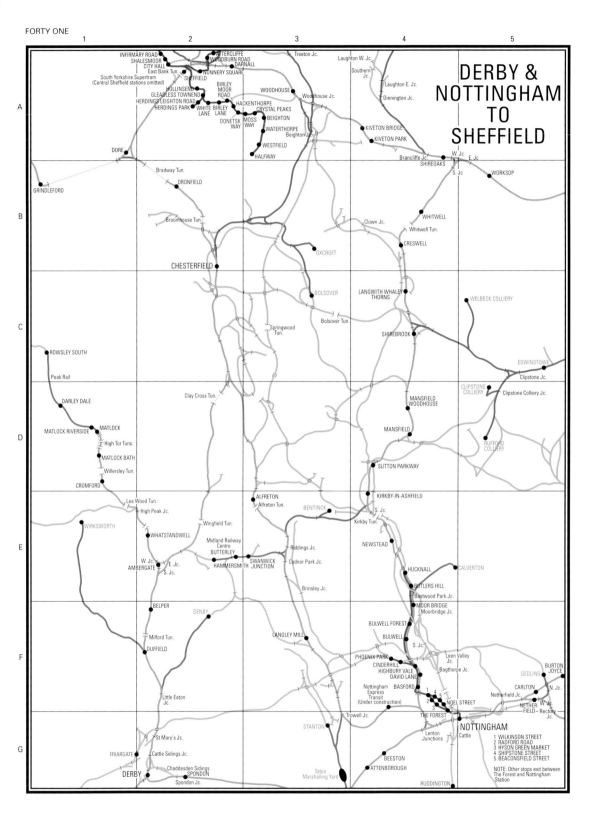

1   2   3   4   5

DERBY & NOTTINGHAM TO SHEFFIELD

INFIRMARY ROAD
SHALESMOOR
CITY HALL
East Bank Tun.
South Yorkshire Supertram
(Central Sheffield stations omitted)
TERCLIFFE
WOODBURN ROAD
DARNALL
NUNNERY SQUARE
SHEFFIELD
HOLLINSEND
GLEADLESS TOWNEND
HERDINGS LEIGHTON ROAD
HERDINGS PARK
WHITE BIRLEY LANE
BIRLEY MOOR ROAD
HACKENTHORPE
CRYSTAL PEAKS
BEIGHTON
DONETSK WAY
MOSS WAY
WATERTHORPE
WESTFIELD
HALFWAY

Treeton Jc.
Laughton W. Jc.
Southern Jc.
Laughton E. Jc.
Dinnington Jc.
WOODHOUSE
Woodhouse Jc.
Beighton Jc.
KIVETON BRIDGE
KIVETON PARK
Brancliffe Jc.   W. Jc   E. Jc
SHIREOAKS   S. Jc.
WORKSOP

A

DORE
Bradway Tun.
DRONFIELD
GRINDLEFORD

Broomhouse Tun.

Clown Jc.
WHITWELL
Whitwell Tun.
CRESWELL

B

OXCROFT
CHESTERFIELD

BOLSOVER
LANGWITH WHALEY THORNS
Bolsover Tun.
SHIREBROOK
WELBECK COLLIERY

C

Springwood Tun.

ROWSLEY SOUTH
Peak Rail
EDWINSTOWE
Clipstone Jc.

DARLEY DALE
Clay Cross Tun.
MANSFIELD WOODHOUSE
CLIPSTONE COLLIERY
Clipstone Colliery Jc.

MATLOCK RIVERSIDE   MATLOCK
High Tor Tuns.
MATLOCK BATH
Willersley Tun.
CROMFORD
MANSFIELD
RUFFORD COLLIERY

D

SUTTON PARKWAY

Lea Wood Tun.
High Peak Jc.
WIRKSWORTH
WHATSTANDWELL
Wingfield Tun.
Midland Railway Centre
BUTTERLEY
SWANWICK JUNCTION
HAMMERSMITH
Riddings Jc.
Codnor Park Jc.
ALFRETON
Alfreton Tun.
BENTINCK
KIRKBY-IN-ASHFIELD
S. Jc.
Kirkby Tun.
NEWSTEAD
CALVERTON

E

W. Jc.   E. Jc.
AMBERGATE   S. Jc.

Brinsley Jc.

HUCKNALL
BUTLERS HILL
Bastwood Park Jc.

BELPER
DENBY
Milford Tun.
DUFFIELD
LANGLEY MILL
MOOR BRIDGE
Moorbridge Jc.
BULWELL FOREST
BULWELL
S. Jc.
Leen Valley Jc.
PHOENIX PARK
CINDERHILL
HIGHBURY VALE
DAVID LANE
Bagthorpe Jc.
BURTON JOYCE
GEDLING
CARLTON
N. Jc.

F

Little Eaton Jc.

Nottingham Express Transit
(Under construction)
BASFORD
1 4
5
2
3
NOEL STREET
Netherfield Jc.
NETHER-
FIELD
W. Jc.
Rectory Jc.

THE FOREST
Trowell Jc.
St Mary's Jc.
STANTON
Lenton Junctions
Cattle
NOTTINGHAM

1 WILKINSON STREET
2 RADFORD ROAD
3 HYSON GREEN MARKET
4 SHIPSTONE STREET
5 BEACONSFIELD STREET

NOTE: Other stops exit between
The Forest and Nottingham
Station

G

FRIARGATE   Cattle Sidings Jc.
DERBY
Chaddesden Sidings
SPONDON
Spondon Jc.
Toton Marshalling Yard
BEESTON
ATTENBOROUGH
RUDDINGTON

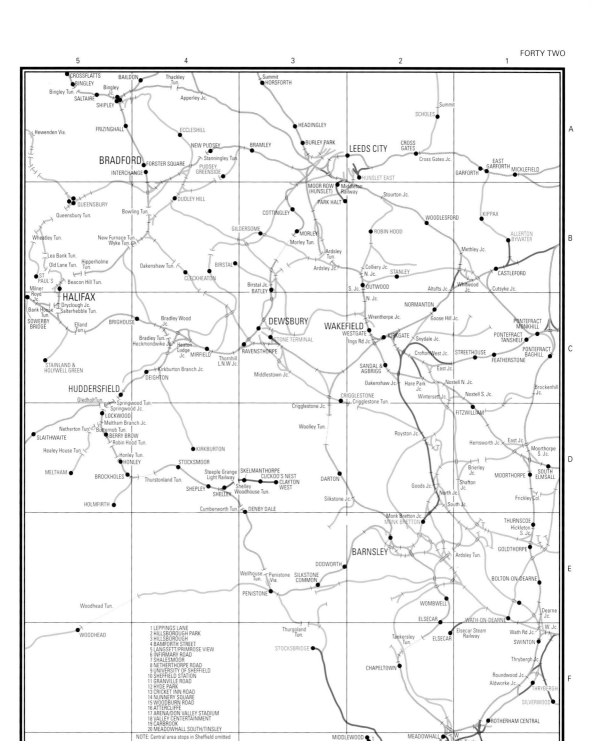

5 4 3 2 1

CROSSFLATTS
BINGLEY
BAILDON Thackley
Tun.
Bingley Tun. Bingley
Jc.
SALTAIRE SHIPLEY Apperley Jc.
Hewenden Via. FRIZINGHALL
ECCLESHILL
Summit
HORSFORTH
HEADINGLEY
BURLEY PARK
A

NEW PUDSEY BRAMLEY LEEDS CITY CROSS GATES Summit
SCHOLES
BRADFORD FORSTER SQUARE Stanningley Tun. Cross Gates Jc. EAST GARFORTH
INTERCHANGE PUDSEY GREENSIDE HUNSLET EAST GARFORTH MICKLEFIELD

QUEENSBURY DUDLEY HILL MOOR ROW (HUNSLET) Middleton Railway Stourton Jc. KIPPAX
Queensbury Tun. Bowling Tun. PARK HALT WOODLESFORD ALLERTON BYWATER B
Wheatley Tun. New Furnace Tun. COTTINGLEY ROBIN HOOD METHLEY Jc.
Lea Bank Tun. Wyke Tun. GILDERSOME MORLEY WOODLESFORD METHLEY Jc.
Old Lane Tun. Hipperholme Tun. Oakenshaw Tun. Morley Tun. STANLEY CASTLEFORD
ST PAUL'S Beacon Hill Tun. CLECKHEATON BIRSTAL Ardsley Tun. Colliery Jc. N. Jc. S. Jc. OUTWOOD Altofts Jc. Whitwood Jc. Cutsyke Jc.
Milner Royd Birstal Jc. BATLEY Ardsley Jc. N. Jc.

HALIFAX Dryclough Jc. Salterhebble Tun. NORMANTON Goose Hill Jc. PONTEFRACT MONKHILL
Bank House Tun. Elland Tun. BRIGHOUSE Bradley Wood Jc. DEWSBURY WAKEFIELD Wrenthorpe Jc. PONTEFRACT TANSHELF
SOWERBY BRIDGE WESTGATE KIRKGATE Snydale Jc. STREETHOUSE PONTEFRACT BAGHILL C
Bradley Tun. Heckmondwike Jc. Heaton Lodge Jc. RAVENSTHORPE DEWSBURY TERMINAL Ings Rd Jc. Crofton West Jc. FEATHERSTONE
STAINLAND & HOLYWELL GREEN Kirkburton Branch Jc. MIRFIELD Thornhill L.N.W Jc. East Jc. Brockenhill Jc.
HUDDERSFIELD DEIGHTON Middlestown Jc. SANDAL & AGBRIGG Oakenshaw Jc. Hare Park Jc. Nostell N. Jc.
GledholtTun. Springwood Tun. CRIGGLESTONE Nostell S. Jc.
Springwood Tun. Crigglestone Jc. Crigglestone Tun. Wintersett Jc.
LOCKWOOD Meltham Branch Jc. FITZWILLIAM
Netherton Tun. Butternob Tun. BERRY BROW Woolley Tun. Royston Jc.
SLAITHWAITE Robin Hood Tun. Hemsworth Jc. East Jc. Moorthorpe S. Jc. D
Healey House Tun. HONLEY KIRKBURTON Brierley Jc. MOORTHORPE SOUTH ELMSALL
MELTHAM BROCKHOLES Thurstonland Tun. STOCKSMOOR Shafton Jc. Frickley Col.
Steeple Grange Light Railway SKELMANTHORPE Goods Jc. North Jc.
SHEPLEY CUCKOO'S NEST CLAYTON WEST DARTON
Shelley Woodhouse Tun. South Jc.
HOLMFIRTH SHELLEY Silkstone Jc.
Cumberworth Jc. DENBY DALE Monk Bretton Jc. THURNSCOE
MONK BRETTON Hickleton S. Jc.
BARNSLEY Ardsley Tun. GOLDTHORPE E
DODWORTH BOLTON-ON-DEARNE
Wellhouse Tun. Penistone Via. SILKSTONE COMMON
PENISTONE WOMBWELL Dearne W. Jc.
WOODHEAD Tun. ELSECAR WATH-ON-DEARNE W. Jc.
Thurgoland Tun. Elsecar Steam Railway Wath Rd Jc.
WOODHEAD 1 LEPPINGS LANE Tankersley Tun. ELSECAR SWINTON
2 HILLSBOROUGH PARK Thrybergh Jc.
3 HILLSBOROUGH STOCKSBRIDGE
4 BAMFORTH STREET Roundwood Jc. F
5 LANGSETT/PRIMROSE VIEW CHAPELTOWN Aldworke Jc.
6 INFIRMARY ROAD THRYBERGH
7 SHALESMOOR SILVERWOOD
8 NETHERTHORPE ROAD
9 UNIVERSITY OF SHEFFIELD
10 SHEFFIELD STATION
11 GRANVILLE ROAD ROTHERHAM CENTRAL
12 HYDE PARK
13 CRICKET INN ROAD MIDDLEWOOD MEADOWHALL W. Jc.
14 NUNNERY SQUARE MALIN BRIDGE Tunnel Jc. E. Tinsley Jc.
15 WOODBURN ROAD TINSLEY YARD
16 ATTERCLIFFE South Yorkshire Supertram
17 ARENA/DON VALLEY STADIUM DARNALL G
18 VALLEY CENTRETAINMENT Treeton Jc.
19 CARBROOK
20 MEADOWHALL SOUTH/TINSLEY SHEFFIELD WOODHOUSE
NOTE: Central area stops in Sheffield omitted

SOUTH WALES

1 CARDIFF (QUEEN ST)
2 CARDIFF (CENTRAL)

ABERGAVENNY

PONTYPOOL & NEW INN
East Jc.
Panteg Jc.
Middle Jc.
South Jc.
CWMBRAN

NEWPORT
Gaer Jc.
Park Jcs.
Mandee Jc.
Pilbrk Jc.
FFOOTS
ALEXANDRA DOCK
Ebbw Jc.

WHISTLE HALT
Pontypool & Blaenavon R. S.
BLAENAVON FURNACE SIDING
Golynos Jc.
Llanhilleth Jc.
Crumlin Viaduct
Cwmbran Jc.
Hall's Tramway Jc.
Risca Jc.

EBBW VALE

RHYMNEY
PONTLOTTYN
PR.-PHIL
BRITHDIR
BARGOED
BULLACH FARGOED
Aber Bargoed Jc.
PENGAM
N. Jc.
S. Jc.
Maesycwm
HENGOED
Sirhowy
Pentar Jc.
S. Jc.
Aber Branch Jc.
East Branch Jc.
West Branch Jc.
Barry Jc.
CAERPHILLY
Caerphilly Tun.
LISVANE & THORNHILL
HEATH HIGH LEVEL
HEATH LOW LEVEL
BIRCHGROVE
RHIWBINA
WHITCHURCH
LLANDAF
CORYTON
Penarth Curve Jcs.
RADYR
FAIRWATER
DANESCOURT
Walnall Jc.
Roath Bch.
Lower Jc.
ABER
Penrhos Jc.
Upper Jc.
Beddau Loop Jc.
NINIAN PARK
WAUN-GRON PARK
GRANGETOWN
Splott Jc.
CARDIFF DOCKS
CATHAYS
DINGLE ROAD
PENARTH
CARDIFF BAY
COGAN
EASTBROOK
DINAS POWYS
CADOXTON
Cadoxton Jc.
BARRY DOCKS
BARRY
BARRY ISLAND
Biglis Jc.
West Jc.
Wenvoe Tun.
Drope Jc.

TREDEGAR
MERTHYR
MERTHYR TYDFIL
PANT
Ivor Jc.
PENTRE-BACH
TROED-Y-RHIW
QUAKERS YARD
Taff Bargoed Jc.
Ystrad Mynach South Jc.
YSTRAD MYNACH
LLANBRADACH
N. Jc.
S. Jc.

PONTSTICILL
Brecon Mountain Railway
TORPANTAU
Torpantau Tun.

ABERDARE
CWMBACH
Mardy Jc.
Dare Valley Jc.
FERNHILL
MOUNTAIN ASH
PENRHIWCEIBER
ABERCYNON NORTH
ABERCYNON SOUTH
Penrhiwgam
Gelly Tarw Jc.
Dare Jc.
Cwmbach Jc.
Penalltia Jc.
TREFOREST
TREFOREST ESTATE
PONTYPRIDD
PORTH
TREHAFOD
Rhondda Bch. Jc.
Tonteg Jc.
Trefngg Railway Jc.
Common Bch. Jc.
CWM
TAFF'S WELL
Maesaraul Jc.
PONTYCLUN
Walnall Jc.
TREHERBERT
YNYSWEN
TREORCHY
TON PENTRE
YSTRAD RHONDDA
LLWYNYPIA
DINAS RHONDDA
TONYPANDY
PONTYGYMMER
Llanelli and District Railway Society
MAESTEG
MAESTEG (EWENNY ROAD)
GARTH
TONDU
SARN
WILDMILL
Coity Jc.
BRIDGEND
W.J. = E.JC.
Cefn Jc.
Bryncethin Jc.
Llantrisant Common Jc.
Mwyndy Jc.
Llanharan Jc.
PENCOED
FORD WORKS
COWBRIDGE
ABERTHAW

Waterhall Jc.
PYLE
PORTHCAWL

CWMGWRACH
ONLLWYN
GWAUN-CAE-GURWEN
Ynys-y-Geinon Jc.
TOWER

NEATH
Court Sart Jc.
Neath Jc.
BRITON FERRY
Aperavon Jc.
BAGLAN
Ton-y-Groes Jcs.
Dyffryn Jc.
PORT TALBOT PARKWAY
Margam Jc.
BAGLAN BAY
SKEWEN
LLANSAMLET
SWANSEA
SIX PITS
GWM HALT Carmel
Swansea Vale RPS Jc.
UPPER BANK
E. JC.
Cockett Tun.
Llangyfelach Tun.

LLANDYBIE
PANTYFFYNNON
Pantyffynnon Jc.
Pantlergaer Tun.
AMMANFORD

5 4 3 2 1

GLASGOW & DISTRICT

A B C D E F G

CUMBERNAULD
GREENFAULDS
CROY
KIRKINTILLOCH
Middlemuir or Monkland Jc.
Woodley Jc.
Campsie Bch. Jc.
LENZIE
Waterside Jc.
Bridgend Jc.
Knightswood Nth. Jc.
WESTERTON
MILNGAVIE
Milngavie Jc.
HILLFOOT
BEARSDEN
SINGER
CLYDEBANK
DRUMCHAPEL
DRUMRY
YOKER
KILPATRICK
DALMUIR
RENFREW
POTTERFIELD
SOUTH
DEANSIDE TRANSIT
PAISLEY
Blackstone Jc.
CART HARBOUR
Walkinshaw Bch. Jc.
GILMOUR STREET
ST. JAMES
Walneuk Jc.
Arkleston Jc.
CANAL
HILLINGTON WEST
HILLINGTON EAST
CARDONALD
MOSSPARK
HAWKHEAD
CROOKSTON
CORKERHILL
Thornly Park Jc.
PRIESTHILL & DARNLEY
NITSHILL
N. Jc.
S. Jc.
POTTERHILL
BARRHEAD
Lyon Cross Jc.
NEILSTON
THORNLIEBANK
KENNISHEAD
GIFFNOCK
Busby Jc.
WILLIAMWOOD
WHITECRAIGS
PATTERTON
CLARKSTON
East Jc.
BUSBY
THORNTONHALL
HAIRMYRES
EAST KILBRIDE
BLANTYRE
Hunthill Jc.
CAMBUSLANG
BURNSIDE
KIRKHILL
Kirkhill Jc.
CROFTFOOT
KING'S PARK
E. Jc.
N. Jc.
CATHCART
Rutherglen Jc.
RUTHERGLEN
LANGSIDE
MUIREND
SHAWLANDS
POLLOKSHAWS EAST
POLLOKSHAWS WEST
MAXWELL PARK
CROSSMYLOOF
QUEENS PARK
POLLOKSHIELDS WEST
POLLOKSHIELDS EAST
Langside Jc.
MOUNT FLORIDA
CROSSHILL
DUMBRECK
IBROX
POLLOKSHIELDS E.
BRIDGETON
DALMARNOCK
BELLGROVE
DUKE STREET
QUEEN STREET
CENTRAL
ARGYLE STREET
ANDERSTON
CHARING CROSS
PARTICK
EXHIBITION CENTRE
HYNDLAND
JORDANHILL
SCOTSTOUNHILL
GARSCADDEN
ANNIESLAND
KELVINSIDE Jc.
Kelvinside Jc.
GILSHOCHILL
MARYHILL
SUMMERSTON
POSSIL PARK & PARKHOUSE
ASHFIELD
BARNHILL
SPRINGBURN
Balornock Jc.
BISHOPBRIGGS
STEPS
Branch Jc.
West Jc.
Milton Jc.
Blackhill Jc.
ALEXANDRA PARADE
CARNTYNE
SPRINGBURN
EASTERHOUSE
SHETTLESTON
GARROWHILL
Tennochside Jc.
MOUNT VERNON
BAILLIESTON
BARGEDDIE
KIRKWOOD
WHIFFLET
CENTRAL
COATBRIDGE
BLAIRHILL
Gartsherrie South Jc.
Gartcosh Jc.
Garnqueen N. Jc.
Garnqueen S. Jc.
Greenside Jc.
SUNNYSIDE
COATDYKE
AIRDRIE
DRUMGELLOCH
Calderbank Bch. Jc.
Dykehead Bch. Jc.
Plains Jc.
Westburn Jc.
CARMYLE
NEWTON
Newton Jc.
UDDINGSTON
Uddingston Jc.
Bothwell Jc.
BOTHWELL
N. Jc.
S. Jc.
BELLSHILL
Fullwood Jcs.
Lanridge Jc.
HOLYTOWN
CARFIN
CLELAND
Omoa Jc.
Chapelknowl Jc.
Dalzell Jc.
SHIELDMUIR
Wishaw Central Jc.
WISHAW
S. Jc.
Strathaven Jc.
Lesmahagow Jc.
MOTHERWELL
AIRBLES
Ross Jc.
HAMILTON WEST
Cadzow Jc.
HAMILTON CENTRAL
Haugh Mead Jc.
Merryton Jc.
FERNIEGAIR
MERRYTON
Eddlewood Jc.
LARKHILL
Stonehouse Jc.

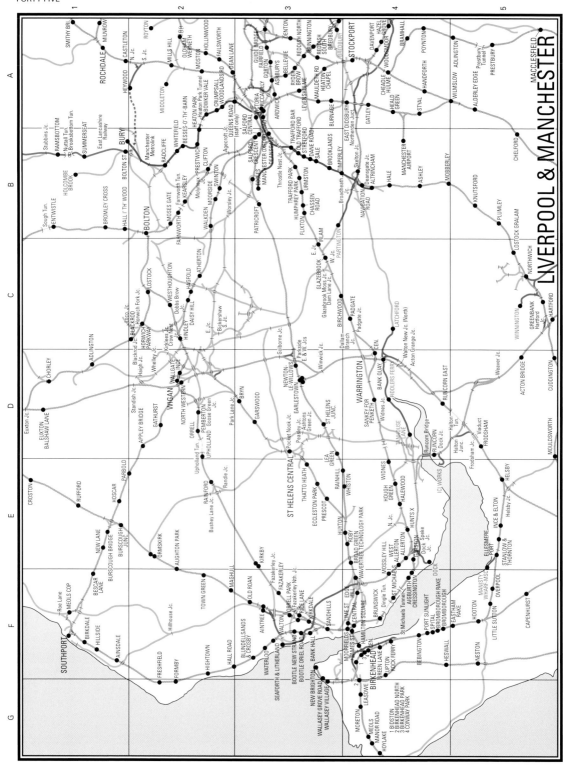

LIVERPOOL & MANCHESTER

INDEX TO PASSENGER STATIONS

Note: Ownership/control of stations is indicated in brackets as follows:

AM	Arriva Trains Merseyside	GW	First Great Western	SL	Silverlink
AN	Arriva Trains Northern	HX	Heathrow Express (BAA)	SR	Scotrail
AR	Anglia Railways	IL	Island Line	SW	South West Trains
CA	Cardiff (part of Wales & Borders)	IoM	Isle of Man	SYS	South Yorkshire Supertram
CC	c2c	LT	London Underground	T&W	Tyne & Wear Metro (Nexus)
CH	Chiltern	ML	Midland Mainline	TL	Thameslink
CT	Central Trains	MM	Midland Metro	TT	Thames Trains
CTL	Croydon Tramlink	MML	Manchester Metrolink	VT	Virgin Trains
DLR	Docklands Light Railway	NET	Nottingham Express Transit	WA	West Anglia Great Northern
ES	Eurostar	NW	First North Western	WB	Wales & Borders
GE	First Great Eastern	Pres	Preservation Society	WE	Wessex Trains
GR	Great North Eastern	RT	Railtrack		
		SC	South Central		
		SE	Connex		

Station	Ref	Station	Ref	Station	Ref	Station	Ref
Abbey Wood (SE)	5B4/40D1	Aldershot (SW)	4B1	Arbroath (SR)	34D3	Attleborough (CT)	12A4/18F4
Aber (CA)	8C4/43B3	Aldgate (LT)	40C4	Ardgay (SR)	36B5	Auchinleck (SR)	29F5
Abercynon North (CA)	8B5/43C3	Aldgate East (LT)	40C4	Ardlui (SR)	32F1	Audley End (WN)	11E4
Abercynon South (CA)	8B5/43C3	Aldrington (SC)	5F3	Ardrossan Harbour (SR)	29D3	Aughton Park (AM)	20B4/24F3/45E2
Aberdare (CA)	8B5/43D2	Alexandra Palace (WN)	40A5	Ardrossan South Beach (SR)	29D3	Avenue Road (CTL)	40F4
Aberdeen (SR)	37G4	Alexandra Parade (SR)	44D4	Ardrossan Town (SR)	29D3	Aviemore (SR)	36F4
Aberdour (SR)	30B3	Alexandria (SR)	29B3	Ardwick (NW)	20B1/45A3	Avoncliff (WB)	3B4
Aberdovey (WB)	13B5	Alfreton (CT)	16C4/41E3	Arena (CTL)	40G4	Avonmouth (WB)	3A2/8C2/9G1
Aberech (WB)	19F1	Allen's West (AN)	28F5	Arena/Don Valley Stadium		Axminster (SW)	2B1
Aberffrwd (Pres)	14C5	Allerton (NW)	45E4	(SYS)	42G2	Aylesbury (CH)	10E2
Abergavenny (WB)	8A3/43A1	Alness (SR)	36C5	Argyle Street (SR)	44E2	Aylesford (SE)	6C5
Abergele & Pensarn (NW)	19D4	Alnmouth (AN)	31F5	Arisaig (SR)	32B5	Aylesham (SE)	6C2
Abergynolwyn (Pres)	13B5	Alperton (LT)	39B2	Arlesey (WN)	11D2	Aylsham (Pres)	18D3
Aberystwyth (WB)	13C5	Alresford (Essex) (GE)	12E4	Arley (Pres)	9A2	Ayr (SR)	29F3
Accrington (NW)	24D1	Alresford (Hants) (Pres)	4C3	Armathwaite (AN)	27D1		
Achanalt (SR)	35D3	Alsager (CT)	15C3/20E1	Arnside (NW)	24A3	Bache (AM)	20D4
Achnasheen (SR)	35D3	Alston (Pres)	27D2	Arram (AN)	22D4	Baglan (WB)	7B4/43F3
Achnashellach (SR)	35D2	Althorne (GE)	6A4/12G5	Arrochar & Tarbet (SR)	32G1	Bagshot (SW)	4B1/5C1
Acklington (AN)	31G5	Althorpe (AN)	22F5	Arundel (SC)	5F1	Baildon (AN)	21D2/42A4
Acle (AR)	18E2	Altnabreac (SR)	38D4	Ascot (SW)	4A1/5B1	Baillieston (SR)	29C5/44C3
Acocks Green (CT)	9A5/15G5	Alton (SW)	4C2	Ascott-under-Wychwood (TT)	10D5	Baker Street (LT)	39C5
Acton Bridge (CT)	15A1/20D2/45B5	Altrincham		Ash (SW)	4B1/5C1	Bala (Pres)	19F4
Acton Central (SL)	39C3	(NW)	15A3/20C1/24G1/45B4	Ash Vale (SW)	4B1/5C1	Balcombe (SC)	5E3
Acton Main Line (TT)	39C3	Alvechurch (CT)	9A4	Ashburys (NW)	20B1/24F1/45A3	Baldock (WN)	11E2
Acton Town (LT)	39D3	Ambergate (CT)	16C5/41E2	Ashchurch (WW)	9D3	Balham (SC)	5B3/39E5
Adderley Park (CT)	13C4/15G5	Amberley (SC)	5F1	Ashey (Pres)	4F3	Ballabeg (IoM)	23C2
Addiewell (SR)	30C4	Amersham (LT)	10F1	Ashfield (SR)	44E4	Ballasalla (IoM)	23C2
Addiscombe (CTL)	40G4	Amlwch (Pres)	19C1/23G1	Ashford (Surrey) (SW)	5B2	Balloch (SR)	29B3
Addlestone (SW)	5C2	Ammanford (WW)	7A3/43G1	Ashford International (SE/ES)	6D4	Balmossie (SR)	34E4
Adisham (SE)	6C2	Ampere Way (CTL)	40G5	Ashley (NW)	15A3/20C1/24G1/45B4	Bamber Bridge (NW)	20A3/24E3
Adlington (Cheshire)		Ancaster (CT)	16C1/17C1	Ashtead (SC)	5C2	Bamford (NW)	15A5
(NW)	15A3/20C1/45A5	Anderston (SR)	44E4	Ashton under Lyne (NW)	21F1	Bamforth Street (SYS)	42G2
Adlington (Lancs)		Andover (SW)	4C4	Ashurst (SC)	5D4	Banavie (SR)	32C3
(NW)	20A2/24E2/45D1	Anerley (SC)	40F4	Ashurst New Forest (SW)	4E4	Banbury (CH)	10C4
Adwick (AN)	21F5	Angel Road (WN)	5A3	Ashwell & Morden (WN)	11D2	Bangor (NW)	19D2
Aigburth (AM)	45F4	Angmering (SC)	5F2	Askam (NW)	24A5	Bank Hall (AM)	45F3
Ainsdale (AM)	20A4/24E4/45F1	Annan (SR)	26B2	Aslockton (CT)	16C2	Bankfoot (T&W)	27B5
Aintree (AM)	20B4/24F4/45F3	Anniesland (SR)	44E4	Aspatria (NW)	26D3	Banstead (SC)	5C3
Airbles (SR)	30C5/44B2	Ansdell & Fairhaven (NW)	20A4/24E4	Aspley Guise (SL)	10C1	Barassie (SR)	29E3
Airdrie (SR)	30C5/44A4	Appleby (AN)	27E2	Aston (CT)	13B4/15G4	Barbican (LT)	40D5
Albany Park (SE)	5B4	Appledore (SC)	6E4	Atherstone (CT)	16F5	Bardon Mill (AN)	27B2
Albrighton (CT)	15F3	Appleford (TT)	10F4	Atherton (NW)	20B2/24F2/45C2	Bare Lane (NW)	24B3
Alderley Edge		Appley Bridge		Attadale (SR)	35D2	Bargeddie (SR)	44C3
(NW)	15A3/20D1/45A5	(NW)	20B3/24F3/45D2	Attenborough (CT)	16D4/41G4	Bargoed (CA)	8B4/43B2
Aldermaston (TT)	4A3	Apsley (SL)	10E1/11F1	Attercliffe (SYS)	41A2/42G2	Barking (CC)	5A4/40B1

Station	Reference
Brockholes (AN)	21F2/42D5
Brockley (SC)	40E3
Brockley Whins (AN)	28C5
Bromborough (AM)	20C4/45F4
Bromborough Rake (AM)	45F4
Bromley by Bow (LT)	40C3
Bromley Cross (NW)	20A2/24E2/45B1
Bromley North (SE)	5B4/40F2
Bromley South (SE)	5B4/40G2
Bromsgrove (CT)	9A4
Brondesbury (SL)	39B4
Brondesbury Park (SL)	39B4
Bronwydd Arms (Pres)	13G4
Brooklands (MML)	20C1/24G1/45B3
Brookmans Park (WN)	11G2
Brookwood (SW)	5C1
Broome (WB)	14C1
Broomfleet (AN)	22E5
Broomhill (Pres)	36F3
Brora (SR)	36A4/38G5
Brough (AN)	22E4
Broughty Ferry (SR)	34E4
Broxbourne (WN)	11F3
Bruce Grove (WN)	40A4
Brundall (AR)	18F2
Brundall Gardens (AR)	18F2
Brunstane (SR)	30G1
Brunswick (AM)	20C4/24G4/45F4
Bruton (WE)	3C3/8F1
Bryn (NW)	20B3/24F3/45D3
Bryn Hynod (Pres)	19F4
Brynglas (Pres)	13B5
Buckenham (AR)	18F2
Buckfastleigh (Pres)	2D4
Buckhurst Hill (LT)	5A4
Buckley (NW)	20D4
Bucknell (WB)	14D1
Bugle (WE)	1D2
Builth Road (WB)	14E3
Bulwell (CT)	16C4/41F4
Bulwell Forest (NET)	41F4
Bungalow (IoM)	23B3
Bures (GE)	12E5
Burgess Hill (SC)	5E3
Burley in Wharfedale (AN)	21C2
Burley Park (AN)	42A3
Burmarsh Road Halt (Pres)	6E3
Burnage (NW)	45A3
Burneside (NW)	27G1
Burnham (TT)	5B1/10G1
Burnham on Crouch (GE)	6A4/12G5
Burnley Barracks (NW)	24D1
Burnley Central (NW)	24D1
Burnley Manchester Road (AN)	24D1
Burnside (SR)	29C5/44D3
Burnt Oak (LT)	5A2
Burntisland (SR)	30A2
Burscough Bridge (NW)	20B4/24F3/45E1
Burscough Junction (NW)	20B4/24F3/45E1
Bursledon (SW)	4E3
Burton Joyce (CT)	16C3/41F5
Burton on Trent (CT)	15E5
Bury (MML)	20B1/24F1/45B1
Bury Bolton Street (Pres)	20B1/24F1/45B1
Bury St Edmunds (AR)	12C5
Busby (SR)	29C5/44E2
Bush Hill Park (WN)	11G3
Bushey (SL)	5A2/11G1
Butlers Hill (NET)	41E4
Butlers Lane (CT)	15F5
Butterley (Pres)	16C5/41E2
Buxted (SC)	5E4
Buxton (Norfolk; Pres)	18E3
Buxton (NW)	15A4
Byfleet & New Haw (SW)	5C1
Byker (T&W)	28A1
Bynea (WB)	7B3
Cadoxton (CA)	8D4/43B5
Caergwrle (NW)	20E4
Caernarfon (Pres)	19D2
Caerphilly (CA)	8C4/43B3
Caersws (WB)	14C3
Caldicot (WB)	8B2/9F1
Caledonian Road & Barnsbury (SL)	40B5
Callerton Parkway (T&W)	27B5
Calstock (WE)	1C5
Cam & Dursley (WE)	8B1/9F2
Camberley (SW)	4B1
Camborne (WE)	1E5
Cambridge (WN)	11C3
Cambridge Heath (WN)	40C4
Camden Road (SL)	40B5
Cambuslang (SR)	29C5/44D3
Camelon (SR)	30B5
Campbells Platform (Pres)	19F3
Canada Water (LT)	40D4
Canley (CT)	10A5
Canning Town (SL)	40C2
Cannock (CT)	15E4
Canonbury (SL)	40B4
Canons Park (LT)	5A2
Canterbury East (SE)	6C3
Canterbury West (SE)	6C3
Cantley (AR)	18F2
Capel Bangor (Pres)	13B5
Capenhurst (AM)	20D4/45F5
Carbis Bay (WE)	1E4
Carbrook (SYS)	42G2
Cardenden (SR)	30A2
Cardiff Bay (CA)	8C4/43B5
Cardiff Central (WB)	8C4/43B4
Cardiff Queen Street (CA)	43B4
Cardonald (SR)	44F3
Cardross (SR)	29B3
Carfin (SR)	44A2
Cark & Cartmel (NW)	24B4
Carlisle (VT)	26C1
Carlton (CT)	16C3/41F5
Carluke (SR)	30D5
Carmarthen (WB)	7A2/13G4
Carmyle (SR)	29C5/44D3
Carnforth (NW)	24B3
Carnoustie (SR)	34E3
Carntyne (SR)	29C5/44D3
Carpenders Park (SL)	5A2
Carrbridge (SR)	36F4
Carrog (Pres)	19F5
Carrog (Pres)	20F5
Carshalton (SC)	5C3
Carshalton Beeches (SC)	5C3
Carstairs (SR)	30D4
Cartsdyke (SR)	29B3
Castle Bar Park (TT)	39C2
Castle Caereinion (Pres)	14B2
Castle Cary (WE)	3C3/8F1
Castle Hedingham (Pres)	11E5
Castleford (AN)	21E4/42B1
Castleton (NW)	20B1/24F1/45A1
Castleton Moor (AN)	28F3
Castletown (IoM)	23C2
Caterham (SC)	5C3
Catford (SC)	40E3
Catford Bridge (SE)	40E3
Cathays (CA)	43B4
Cathcart (SR)	29C5/44E3
Cattal (AN)	21C4
Causeland (WW)	1D4
Cefn-y-Bedd (NW)	20E4
Chadwell Heath (GE)	5A4
Chafford Hundred (CC)	5B5
Chalfont & Latimer (LT)	10F1
Chalkwell (CC)	6A4
Chapel-en-le-Frith (NW)	15A4
Chapleton (WE)	7F3
Chapeltown (AN)	21F3/42F2
Chappel & Wakes Colne (GE)	12E5
Charing (SE)	6C4
Charing Cross (Glasgow) (SR)	44E4
Charlbury (TT)	10D5
Charlton (SE)	5B4/40D2
Chartham (SE)	6C3
Chassen Road (NW)	45B3
Chatham (SE)	6B5
Chathill (AN)	31E5
Cheadle Hulme (NW)	15A3/20C1/24G1/45A4
Cheam (SC)	5C3
Cheddington (SL)	10E1
Cheddleton (Pres)	15C4
Chelford (NW)	15A3/20D1/45B5
Chelmsford (GE)	11F5
Chelsfield (SE)	5C4
Cheltenham Racecourse (Pres)	9D4
Cheltenham Spa (WE)	9D3
Chepstow (WB)	8B29F1
Cherry Tree (NW)	20A2/24E2
Chertsey (SW)	5B1
Chesham (LT)	10F1
Cheshunt (WN)	11G3
Chessington North (SW)	5C2
Chessington South (SW)	5C2
Chester (NW)	20D4
Chester le Street (AN)	27C5
Chester Road (CT)	15F5
Chesterfield (ML)	16A5/41C2
Chestfield & Swalecliffe (SE)	6B3
Chetnole (WE)	8E2
Chichester (SC)	4E1
Chichester (T&W)	9D4
Chigwell (LT)	5A4
Chilham (SE)	6C3
Chillingham Road (T&W)	28A1
Chilworth (TT)	5D1
Chingford (WN)	11G3
Chinley (NW)	15A4
Chinnor (Pres)	10F2
Chippenham (GW)	3A4
Chipstead (SC)	5C3
Chislehurst (SE)	5B4/40F2
Chirk (WB)	20F4
Chiswick (SC)	39D3
Chiswick Park (LT)	39D3
Cholsey (TT)	10F4
Chorley (NW)	20A3/24E2/45D1
Chorleywood (LT)	5A1/10F1/11G1
Christchurch (SW)	4F5
Christs Hospital (SC)	5E2
Church & Oswaldtwistle (NW)	24D1
Church Fenton (AN)	21D4
Church Stretton (WB)	14B1/15F1
Churston (Pres)	2D3
Cilmeri (WB)	14E3
Cinderhill (NET)	41F4
City Hall (SYS)	41A2
Clacton (GE)	12F3
Clandon (SW)	5C1
Clapham (AN)	24B1
Clapham High Street (SC)	40E5
Clapham Junction (SW)	5B3/39E5
Clapton (WN)	40B4
Clarbeston Road (WB)	13G1
Clarkston (SR)	29C5/44E2
Claverdon (CT)	9B5
Claygate (SW)	5C2
Clayton West (Pres)	21F3/42D3
Cleethorpes (AN)	22F2
Cleland (SR)	30C5/44A2
Clifton (NW)	20B1/24F1/45B2
Clifton Down (WE)	3A2/8C2/9G1
Clitheroe (NW)	24D1
Clock House (SE)	40F4
Clunderwen (WB)	13G2
Clydebank (SR)	44F4
Coatbridge (SR)	44B4
Coatbridge Sunnyside (SR)	44B4
Coatdyke (SR)	44B4
Cobham & Stoke d'Abernon (SW)	5C2
Cockfosters (LT)	5A3
Codsall (CT)	15F3
Cogan (CA)	8C4/43B5
Colby (IoM)	23C2
Colby Level (IoM)	23C2
Colchester (GE)	12E4
Colchester Town (GE)	12E4
Coleslogett Halt (Pres)	1D3
Colindale (LT)	39A3
Colliers Wood (LT)	39F5
Collingham (CT)	16B2
Collington (SC)	6F5

Horley (SC)	5D3	Inverness (SR)	36E5
Hornbeam Park (AN)	21C3	Invershin (SR)	35A5
Hornsey (WN)	40A5	Inverurie (SR)	37F3
Horsforth (AN)	21D3/42A3	Ipswich (AR)	12D4

Kinbrace (SR) 38E5 — Langsett/Primrose View (SYS) 42G2

Horley (SC) 5D3
Hornbeam Park (AN) 21C3
Hornsey (WN) 40A5
Horsforth (AN) 21D3/42A3
Horsham (SC) 5E2
Horsley (SW) 5C2
Horsted Keynes (Pres) 5E3
Horton in Ribblesdale (AN) 24B1
Horwich Parkway
  (NW) 20B2/24F2/45C2
Hoscar (NW) 20B3/24F3/45E1
Hough Green
  (NW) 15A1/20C3/24G3/45E4
Hounslow (SW) 5B239E1
Hounslow Central (LT) 39D1
Hounslow East (LT) 39D1
Hounslow West (LT) 39D1
Hoveton & Wroxham (AR) 18E2
Hove (SC) 5F3
How Wood (SL) 11G1
Howden (AN) 22E5
Howdon (T&W) 28B5
Howwood (SR) 29C4
Hoylake (AM) 20C5/24G5/45G4
Hubbert's Bridge (CT) 17C2
Hucknall (CT) 16C4/41E4
Huddersfield (AN) 21E2/42C5
Hull (AN) 22E3
Humphrey Park (NW) 45B3
Huncoat (NW) 24D1
Hungerford (TT) 4A4
Hunmanby (AN) 22B3
Huntingdon (WN) 11B2
Huntly (SR) 37E1
Hunts Cross (AM) 45E4
Hurst Green (SC) 5C4
Hutton Cranswick (AN) 22C4
Huyton (NW) 20C3/24G3/45E4
Hyde Central (NW) 21G1
Hyde North (NW) 21G1
Hyde Park (SYS) 42G2
Hykeham (CT) 16B1
Hyndland (SR) 44E4
Hyson Green Market (NET) 41F4
Hythe (GE) 12E4
Hythe (Pres) 6D3

IBM (SR) 29B3
Ibrox (SR) 44E3
Ickenham (LT) 5A2
Ifield (SC) 5D3
Ilford (GE) 5A4/40B1
Ilford Road (T&W) 27B5
Ilkley (AN) 21C2
Ince (NW) 45D2
Ince & Elton (NW) 15A1/20D3/45E5
Infirmary Road (SYS) 41A2/42G2
Ingatestone (GE) 11G4
Ingrow West (Pres) 21D1
Insch (SR) 37E2
Invergordon (SR) 36C5
Invergowrie (SR) 34E5
Inverkeithing (SR) 30B3
Inverkip (SR) 29C2

Inverness (SR) 36E5
Invershin (SR) 35A5
Inverurie (SR) 37F3
Ipswich (AR) 12D4
Irlam (NW) 20C2/24G2/45C3
Irton Road (Pres) 26F3
Irvine (SR) 29E3
Irwell Vale (Pres) 20A1/24E1
Isfield (Pres) 5F4
Isleworth (SW) 39D2
Islip (TT) 10E4
Iver (TT) 5B1/10G1
Ivybridge (WE) 2D5

Jarrow (T&W) 28B5
Jesmond (T&W) 27B5/28A1
Jewellery Quarter (CT) 13C3
Johnston (WB) 7C1
Johnstone (SR) 29C4
Jordanhill (SR) 44E4

Kearsley (NW) 20B2/24F1/45B2
Kearsney (SE) 6D2
Keighley (AN) 21D1
Keith (SR) 37D1
Keith Town (Pres) 37D1
Kelling Heath Park (Pres) 18D4
Kelvedon (GE) 12F5
Kemble (WE) 9F4
Kempston Hardwick (SL) 10C1/11D1
Kemsing (SE) 5C5
Kemsley (SE) 6B4
Kendal (NW) 24A3/27G1
Kenley (SC) 5C3
Kennett (AR) 11C5
Kennishead (SR) 44E3
Kenrick Park (MM) 13B2
Kensal Green (SL) 39B4
Kensal Rise (SL) 39B4
Kensington Olympia (SL) 5B3/39D4
Kent House (SE) 40F4
Kent's Bank (NW) 24B4
Kentish Town (TL) 40B5
Kentish Town West (SL) 40B5
Kenton (SL) 39A2
Kettering (ML) 10A2
Kew Bridge (SW) 39D3
Kew Gardens (SL) 39D3
Keyham (WE) 1D5
Keynsham (WE) 3A3/8D1
Kidbrooke (SE) 5B4/40E2
Kidderminster (CT) 9A3
Kidderminster Town (Pres) 9A3
Kidsgrove (CT) 15C3/20E1
Kidwelly (WB) 7A2
Kilburn (LT) 39B4
Kilburn High Road (SL) 39B5
Kildale (AN) 28F3
Kildonan (SR) 38F5
Kilgetty (WB) 7D3
Kilmarnock (SR) 29E4
Kilmaurs (SR) 29E4
Kilpatrick (SR) 29B4/44G5
Kilwinning (SR) 29D3

Kinbrace (SR) 38E5
Kingham (TT) 9D5
Kinghorn (SR) 30A2
Kings Langley (SL) 10G1/11G1
King's Lynn (WN) 17E4
Kings Norton (CT) 9A4
Kings Nympton (WE) 7G4
Kings Park (SR) 44D3
Kings Sutton (CH) 10C4
Kingsbury (LT) 39A3
Kingscote (Pres) 5D3
Kingsknowe (SR) 30B2
Kingsley & Froghall (Pres) 15C4
Kingston (SW) 5B2/39F2
Kingston Park (T&W) 27B5
Kingswear (Pres) 2D3
Kingswood (SC) 5C3
Kingussie (SR) 33A2
Kinneil (Pres) 30B4
Kintbury (TT) 4A4
Kirby Cross (GE) 12E3
Kirk Sandall (AN) 21F5
Kirkaldy (SR) 30A2
Kirkby (AM) 20B4/24F3/45E3
Kirkby in Ashfield (CT) 16C4/41E4
Kirkby in Furness (NW) 24A5
Kirkby Stephen (AN) 27F2
Kirkconnel (SR) 30F5
Kirkdale (AM) 45F3
Kirkham & Wesham (NW) 24D3
Kirkhaugh (Pres) 27C2
Kirkhill (SR) 29C5/44D2
Kirknewton (SR) 30C3
Kirkwood (SR) 44B3
Kirton Lindsey (AN) 22F4
Kiveton Bridge (AN) 16A4/41A4
Kiveton Park (AN) 16A4/41A4
Knaresborough (AN) 21C3
Knebworth (WN) 11E2
Knighton (WB) 14D2
Knockholt (SE) 5C4
Knottingley (AN) 21E4
Knucklas (WB) 14D2
Knutsford (NW) 15A2/20D2/45B5
Kyle of Lochalsh (SR) 35F1

Ladbroke Grove (LT) 39C4
Ladybank (SR) 34F5
Ladywell (SE) 40E3
Laindon (CC) 5A5
Lairg (SR) 35A5
Lake (IL) 4F3
Lakenheath (CT) 11A5/17G5
Lakeside (Pres) 24A3/26G1
Lamphey (WB) 7D2
Lanark (SR) 30D4
Lancaster (VT) 24C3
Lancing (SC) 5F2
Landywood (CT) 15E4
Langbank (SR) 29B3
Langho (NW) 24D2
Langley (TT) 5B1/10G1
Langley Green (CT) 13C2/15G4
Langley Mill (CT) 16C4/41F3

Langsett/Primrose View (SYS) 42G2
Langside (SR) 44E3
Langwathby (AN) 27D1
Langwith-Whaley Thorns
  (CT) 16B4/41C4
Lapford (WE) 2A4
Lapworth (CT) 9A5
Larbert (SR) 30B5
Largs (SR) 29C2
Larkhall (SR) 30D5/44B1
Latimer Road (LT) 39C4
Launceston (Pres) 1B4
Lawrence Hill (WE) 3A2
Laxey (IoM) 23B3
Layton (NW) 24D4
Lazonby & Kirkoswald (AN) 27D1
Lea Green (NW) 20C3/24G3/45D3
Lea Hall (CT) 15G5
Leadhills (Pres) 30F4
Leagrave (TL) 10D1/11E1
Lealholm (AN) 28F3
Leamington Spa (CT) 10B5
Leasowe (AM) 20C5/24G5/45G4
Leatherhead (SC) 5C2
Ledbury (CT) 9C2
Lee (SE) 5B4/40E2
Leeds (RT) 21D3/42A2
Leicester (ML) 16F3
Leicester North (Pres) 16E3
Leigh (SE) 5D5
Leigh on Sea (CC) 6A5
Leighton Buzzard (SL) 10D1
Lelant (WE) 1E4
Lelant Saltings (WE) 1E4
Lenham (SE) 6C4
Lenzie (SR) 29B5/44D5
Leominster (WB) 9B1
Leppings Lane (SYS) 42G2
Letchworth (WN) 11E2
Leuchars for St Andrews (SR) 34F4
Levenshulme (NW) 20C1/24G1/45A3
Levisham (Pres) 22A5/28G2
Lewes (SC) 5F4
Lewisham (SC) 40E3
Leyland (NW) 20A3/24E3
Leyton (LT) 40B3
Leyton Midland Road (SL) 40B3
Leytonstone (LT) 5A4/40A2
Leytonstone High Road (SL) 40B2
Lichfield City (CT) 15E5
Lichfield Trent Valley (CT) 15E5
Lidlington (SL) 10C1
Limehouse (CC) 40C3
Lincoln (CT) 16B1/17B1
Lingfield (SC) 5D4
Lingwood (AR) 18F2
Linlithgow (SR) 30B4
Liphook (SW) 4D1
Liskeard (WE) 1D4
Liss (SW) 4D1
Lisvane & Thornhill (CA) 8C4/43B4
Little Kimble (CH) 10E2
Little Sutton (AM) 20D4/45F5
Littleborough (AN) 21E1

Station	Ref
Phoenix Park (NET)	16C4
Pickering (Pres)	22A5
Pilning (WE)	8C2/9G1
Pinhoe (SW)	2C3
Pinner (LT)	39A1
Pitlochry (SR)	33C4
Pitsea (CC)	6A5
Pitsford (Pres)	10B2
Plaistow (LT)	40C2
Plas Halt (Pres)	19F3
Pleasington (NW)	20A2/24E2
Plockton (SR)	35E1
Pluckley (SE)	6D4
Plumley (NW)	15A2/20D2/45B5
Plumpton (SC)	5F3
Plumstead (SE)	40D1
Plymouth (GW)	1D5
Pokesdown (SW)	4F5
Polegate (SC)	5F5
Polesworth (CT)	16F5
Pollokshaws East (SR)	44E3
Pollokshaws West (SR)	44E3
Pollokshields East (SR)	44E3
Pollokshields West (SR)	44E3
Polmont (SR)	30B4
Polsloe Bridge (WE)	2B3
Ponders End (WN)	11G3
Pont Croesor (Pres)	19F2
Pontarddulais (WB)	7A3
Pontefract Baghill (AN)	21E4/42C1
Pontefract Monkhill (AN)	21E4/42C1
Pontefract Tanshelf (AN)	21E4/42C1
Pontlottyn (CA)	8A5/43C2
Pontsticill (Pres)	8A5/43C1
Pontyclun (WB)	8C5/43C4
Pontycymmer (Pres)	7B5
Pont-y-Pant (NW)	19E3
Pontypool & New Inn (WB)	8B3/43A2
Pontypridd (CA)	8B5/43C3
Poole (SW)	3F5
Poppleton (AN)	21C4
Port Erin (IoM)	23C1
Port Glasgow (SR)	29B3
Port Soderick (IoM)	23C2
Port St Mary (IoM)	23C1
Port Sunlight (AM)	45F4
Port Talbot Parkway (WB)	7B4/43F3
Portchester (SW)	4E3
Porth (CA)	8B5/43C3
Porthmadog (WB)	19F2
Portlethen (SR)	34A1/37G4
Portslade (SC)	5F3
Purley (SC)	5C3
Portsmouth & Southsea (SW)	4E2
Portsmouth Arms (WW)	7G3
Portsmouth Harbour (SW)	4E2
Possilpark & Parkhouse (SR)	44E4
Potters Bar (WN)	11G2
Poulton-le-Fylde (NW)	24D4
Poynton (NW)	15A3/20C1/45A4
Prees (WB)	15D1/20F3
Prescot (NW)	20C3/24G3/45E3
Prestatyn (NW)	19C5
Prestbury (NW)	15A3/20D1/45A5

Station	Ref
Preston (VT)	20A3/24D3
Preston Park (SC)	5F3
Preston Road (LT)	39A3
Prestonpans (SR)	30B1
Prestwich (MML)	20B1/24F1/45B2
Prestwick International Airport (SR)	29E3
Prestwick Town (SR)	29E3
Priestfield (Midland Metro)	13A1/15E3
Priesthill & Darnley (SR)	44F3
Princes Risborough (CH)	10F2
Prittlewell (GE)	6A4
Prudhoe (AN)	27C4
Pudding Mill Lane (DLR)	40B3
Pulborough (SC)	5E1
Purfleet (CC)	5B5
Purley Oaks (SC)	5C3
Putney (SW)	5B3/39E4
Putney Bridge (LT)	39E4
Pwllheli (WB)	19F1
Pyle (WB)	7C5/43E4
Quakers Yard (CA)	8B5/43C2
Queenborough (SE)	6B4
Queens Park (London) (SL)	39B5
Queens Park (SR)	44E3
Queens Road (Peckham) (SC)	40D4
Queensbury (LT)	39A3
Queenstown Road (SW)	39D5
Quellyn Lake (Pres)	19E2
Quintrell Downs (WE)	1D1
Quorn & Woodhouse (Pres)	16E4
Radcliffe (CT)	16D3
Radcliffe (MML)	20B1/24F1/45B2
Radford Road (NET)	41F4
Radlett (TL)	11G1
Radley (TT)	10F4
Radstock (Pres; prop)	3B3/8E1
Radyr (CA)	8C4/43C4
Rainford (NW)	20B3/24F3/45E2
Rainham (Essex) (GE)	5A4
Rainham (Kent) (SE)	6B5
Rainhill (NW)	20C3/24G3//45E4
Ramsbottom (Pres)	20A1/24E1/45B1
Ramsey (IoM)	23B3/25G4
Ramsgate (SE)	6B1
Ramsgreave & Wilpshire (NW)	24D2
Rannoch (SR)	32D1/33C1
Rauceby (CT)	16C1/17C1
Ravenglass (NW)	26G3
Ravenglass (Pres)	26G3
Ravensbourne (SE)	40F3
Ravenscourt Park (LT)	39D4
Ravensthorpe (AN)	21E3/42C3
Rawcliffe (AN)	21E5
Rawtenstall (Pres)	20A1/24E1
Rayleigh (GE)	6A5
Rayners Lane (LT)	39B1
Raynes Park (SW)	5B3/39F4
Reading (GW)	4A2
Reading West (TT)	4A2
Rectory Road (WN)	40B4
Redbridge (LT)	40A2

Station	Ref
Redbridge (SW)	4E4
Redcar Central (AN)	28E3
Redcar East (AN)	28E3
Reddish North (NW)	45A3
Reddish South (NW)	45A3
Redditch (CT)	9A4
Redhill (SC)	5C3
Redland (WE)	3A2
Redruth (WE)	1E5
Reedham (AR)	18F2
Reedham (Surrey) (SC)	5C3
Regent Centre (T&W)	27B5
Reigate (SC)	5C3
Renton (SR)	29B3
Retford (GR)	16A3
Rheidol Falls (Pres)	14C5
Rhiwbina (CA)	43B4
Rhosneigr (NW)	19B2/19D1
Rhydyronen (Pres)	13B5
Rhyl (NW)	19C5
Rhymney (CA)	8A5/43C1
Ribblehead (AN)	24A1
Rice Lane (AM)	45A3
Richmond (SW)	5B2/39E3
Rickmansworth (LT)	5A2/10F1/11G1
Riddlesdown (SC)	5C3
Ridgmont (SL)	10C1
Riding Mill (AN)	27C4
Rishton (NW)	24D2
Robertsbridge (SE)	6F5
Roby (NW)	20C4/24G3/45E4
Rochdale (NW)	20B1/21G2/45A1
Roche (WE)	1D2
Rochester (SE)	6B5
Rochford (GE)	6A4
Rock Ferry (AM)	20C4/24G4/45F4
Roding Valley (LT)	5A4
Rogart (SR)	36A5
Rolleston (CT)	16C2
Rolvenden (Pres)	6E4
Roman Bridge (NW)	19E3
Romford (GE)	5A4
Romiley (NW)	21G1
Romney Sands (Pres)	6E3
Romsey (WE)	4D4
Ronaldsway Halt (IoM)	23C2
Roose (NW)	24B5
Ropley (Pres)	4C2
Rose Grove (NW)	24D1
Rose Hill Marple (NW)	21G1
Rosyth (SR)	30B3
Rotherham Central (AN)	21G4/42F1
Rotherhithe (LT)	40D4
Rothley (Pres)	16E4
Roughton Road (SR)	18D3
Rowland's Castle (SW)	4E2
Rowley Regis (CT)	13C2/15G4
Rowsley South (Pres)	16B5/41C1
Royal Oak (LT)	39C5
Roy Bridge (SR)	32B2
Roydon (WN)	11F3
Royston (WN)	11D3
Ruabon (WB)	20F4
Ruddington (Pres)	16D3

Station	Ref
Rufford (NW)	20A3/24E3/45E1
Rugby (VT)	10A4
Rugeley Town (CT)	15E4
Rugeley Trent Valley (CT)	15E4
Ruislip Manor (LT)	5A2
Runcorn (VT)	15A1/20C3/45D4
Runcorn East (NW)	15A1/20C3/45D4
Ruskington (CT)	17C1
Ruswarp (AN)	28F2
Rutherglen (SR)	29C5/44D3
Ryde Espanade (IL)	4F3
Ryde Pierhead (IL)	4F3
Ryde St Johns Road (IL)	4F3
Ryder Brow (NW)	45A3
Rye (SC)	6E4
Rye House (WN)	11F3
St Albans (TL)	11F1
St Albans Abbey (SL)	11F1
St Andrews Road (WE)	8C2/9G1
St Anne's-on-the-Sea (NW)	24D4
St Austell (WE)	1D2
St Bees (NW)	26F4
St Budeaux Ferry Road (WE)	1D5
St Budeaux Victoria Road (WE)	1D5
St Columb Road (WE)	1D2
St Denys (SW)	4D4
St Erth (WE)	1F4
St Germans (WE)	1D5
St Helens Central (NW)	20C3/24G3/45D3
St Helens Junction (NW)	20C3/24G3/45D3
St Helier (SW)	39G4
St Ives (WE)	1E4
St James (T&W)	28A2
St James Park (WE)	2B3
St James' Park (LT)	40D5
St James Street (WN)	40A3
St Johns (SE)	40E3
St Johns Wood (LT)	39B5
St Keyne (WE)	1D4
St Leonards Warrior Square (SE)	6F5
St Margarets (Herts) (WN)	11F3
St Margarets (SW)	39E2
St Mary Cray (SE)	5B4/40G1
St Marys Halt (Pres)	8A1/9E2
St Michaels (AM)	45F5
St Neots (WN)	11C2
St Pauls (Midland Metro)	13C3
St Peters (T&W)	28C5
Sale (MML)	20C1/24G1/45B3
Salem (Pres)	19E2
Salford Central (NW)	20B1/24F1/45B2
Salford Crescent (NW)	45B2
Salfords (SC)	5D3
Salhouse (AR)	18E2
Salisbury (SW)	4C5
Saltaire (AN)	21D2/42A5
Saltash (WE)	1D5
Saltburn (AN)	28E3
Saltcoats (SR)	29E3
Saltford (Pres)	3A3/8D1
Saltmarshe (AN)	22E5

Sunbury (SW) 5B2
Sunderland (AN) 28C5
Sundridge Park (SE) 40F2
Sunningdale (SW) 5B1
Sunnymeads (SW) 5B1
Surbiton (SW) 5B2/39G2
Surrey Quays (LT) 40D4
Sutton (SC) 5C3
Sutton Coldfield (CT) 15F5
Sutton Common (TL) 39G4
Sutton Parkway (CT) 16B4/41D4
Swale (SE) 6B4
Swanage (Pres) 3G5
Swanley (SE) 5B4
Swanscombe (SE) 5B5
Swansea (GW) 7B4/43G3
Swanwick (SW) 4E3
Swanwick Junction (Pres) 41E3
Sway (SW) 4E5
Swaythling (SW) 4D4
Swinderby (CT) 16B2
Swindon (GW) 9G5
Swindon (Moredon) (Pres) 9F5
Swineshead (CT) 17C2
Swinton (NW) 20B1/24F1/45B2
Swinton (AN) 21F4/42F1
Swiss Cottage (LT) 39B5
Sydenham (SC) 40F4
Sydenham Hill (SE) 40F4
Sylfaen (Pres) 14B2
Syon Lane (SW) 39D2
Syston (CT) 16E3

Tackley (TT) 10D4
Tadworth (SC) 5C3
Taff's Well (CA) 8C4/43C4
Tain (SR) 36B4
Tal-y-Cafn (NW) 19D4
Talsarnau (WB) 19F2
Talybont (WB) 13A5/19G2
Tame Bridge Parkway (CT) 13B3/15F4
Tamworth (CT) 15F5
Tan-y-Bwlch (Pres) 19F3
Tan-y-Grisiau (Pres) 19F3
Taplow (TT) 5B1/10G2
Tattenham Corner (SC) 5C3
Taunton (GW) 8F4
Taynuilt (SR) 32E3
Tebay 27F1
Teddington (SW) 5B2/39F2
Tees-side Airport (AN) 28F5
Teignmouth (WE) 2C3
Telford Central (CT) 15F2
Temple (LT) 40D5
Templecombe (SW) 3D3/8G1
Tenby (WB) 7D3
Tenterden Town (Pres) 6D4
Terminal 4 (HX) 5B2
Teynham (SE) 6C4
Thames Ditton (SW) 5B239G2
Thatcham (TT) 4A3
Thatto Heath (NW) 20C3/24G3/45E3
The Crescent (Midland Metro) 13A1

The Forest (NET) 41F4
The Green (Pres) 26F2
The Hawthorns (CT) 13B3
The Lakes (CT) 9A5
The Midden (Pres) 18C5
The Royal (Midland Metro) 15E3
Theale (TT) 4A2
Theobald's Grove (WN) 11G3
Therapia Lane (CTL) 40G5
Thetford (CT) 12A5/18G5
Theydon Bois (LT) 11G3
Thirsk (AN) 21A4
Thornaby (AN) 28E4
Thorne North (AN) 21E5
Thorne South (AN) 21F5
Thornford (WE) 3E2
Thornliebank (SR) 29C5/44E2
Thornton Abbey (AN) 22E3
Thornton Heath (SC) 5B3/40G5
Thorntonhall (SR) 29D5/44E2
Thorpe Bay (CC) 6A4
Thorpe Culvert (CT) 17B4
Thorpe-le-Soken (GE) 12E3
Three Bridges (SC) 5D3
Three Oaks (SC) 6F5
Thurgarton (CT) 16C3
Thurnscoe (AN) 21F4/42E1
Thurso (SR) 38C3
Thurston (AR) 12C5
Tilbury Town (CC) 5B5
Tile Hill (CT) 10A5
Tilehurst (TT) 4A2/10G3
Timperley (MML) 20C1/24G1/45B3
Tipton (CT) 13B2/15F4
Tirphil (CA) 8B4/43B2
Tisbury (SW) 3D4
Tiverton Parkway (GW) 2A2/8G5
Toddington (Pres) 9D4
Todmorden (AN) 20A1/21E1
Tolworth (SW) 5C2/39G3
Ton Pentre (CA) 8B5/43D2
Tonbridge (SE) 5D5
Tondu (WB) 7C5/43D4
Tonfanau (WB) 13B5
Tonypandy (CA) 8B5/43D3
Tooting (TL) 39F5
Tooting Bec (LT) 39G5
Tooting Broadway (LT) 39F5
Topsham (WE) 2B3
Torpantau (Pres) 8A5/43C1
Torquay (WE) 2D3
Torre (WE) 2D3
Totnes (GW) 2D4
Totnes (Littlehempston) (Pres) 2D4
Tottenham Hale (WN) 40A4
Totteridge (LT) 5A3/11G2
Totton (SW) 4E4
Town Green (AM) 20B4/24F4/45F2
Trafford Bar (MML) 45B3
Trafford Park (NW) 20C1/24G1/45B3
Trefforest (CA) 8B5/43C3
Trefforest Estate (CA) 8C5/43C3
Trehafod (CA) 8B5/43C3
Treherbert (CA) 8B5/43D2

Treorchy (CA) 8B5/43D2
Trimley (AR) 12E3
Tring (SL) 10E1
Trinity Way (Midland Metro) 13B2
Troed-y-Rhiw (CA) 8B5/43C2
Troon (SR) 29E3
Trowbridge (WE) 3B4
Truro (WE) 1E1
Tulloch (SR) 32B1
Tulse Hill (SC) 5B340E5
Tunbridge Wells (SE) 5D5
Tunbridge Wells West (Pres) 5D5
Turkey Street (WN) 11G3
Turnham Green (LT) 39D3
Tutbury & Hatton (CT) 15D5
Twickenham (SW) 5B2/39E2
Twyford (TT) 4A1/10G2
Ty Croes (NW) 19D1
Ty Glas (CA) 43B4
Tygwyn (WB) 19F2
Tyndrum Lower (SR) 32E1
Tyne Dock (T&W) 28B5
Tynemouth (T&W) 28B5
Tyseley (CT) 15G5
Tywyn (WB) 13B5
Tywyn Pendre (Pres) 13B5
Tywyn Wharf (Pres) 13B5

Uckfield (SC) 5E4
Uddingston (SR) 29C5/44C3
Ulceby (AN) 22E3
Ulleskelf (AN) 21D4
Ulverston (NW) 24A4
Umberleigh (WE) 7F3
University (CT) 13C3/15G4
University of Sheffield (SYS) 42G2
Uphall (SR) 30C3
Upholland (NW) 20B3/24F3/45D2
Upminster (CC) 5A5
Upper Bank (Pres) 43G3
Upper Halliford (SW) 5B2
Upper Holloway (SL) 40B5
Upper Tyndrum (SR) 32E1
Upper Warlingham (SC) 5C3
Upton (NW) 20C4/24G4/45F4
Upton Park (LT) 40B2
Upwey (SW) 3G3
Urmston (NW) 20C1/24G1/45B3
Uttoxeter (CT) 15D5
Uxbridge (LT) 5A2/10G1

Valley (NW) 19B2
Valley Centertainment (SYS) 42G2
Vauxhall (SW) 40D5
Virginia Water (SW) 5B1

Waddon (SC) 5C3
Waddon Marsh (CTL) 40G5
Wadhurst (SE) 5E5
Wainfleet (CT) 17C4
Wainhill (Pres) 10F2
Wakefield Kirkgate (AN) 21E3/42C2
Wakefield Westgate (GR) 21E3/42C2
Walkden (NW) 20B2/24F1/45B2

Wallasey Grove Road (AM) 20C4/24G4/45F4
Wallasey Village (AM) 20C4/24G4/45F4
Wallingford (Pres) 10F3
Wallington (SC) 5C3
Wallsend (T&W) 28B5
Wallyford (SR) 30B2
Walmer (SE) 6C1
Walsall (CT) 15F4
Walsden (AN) 21E1
Walsingham (Pres) 18D5
Waltham Cross (WN) 11G3
Walthamstow Central (WN) 40A3
Walthamstow Queens Road (SL) 40A3
Walton on Naze (GE) 12E3
Walton on Thames (SW) 5C2
Walton (AM) 45F3
Wanborough (SW) 5C1
Wandsworth Common (SC) 39E5
Wandsworth Road (SC) 40E5
Wandsworth Town (SW) 39E5
Wansbeck (T&W) 27B5
Wansford (Pres) 11A1/17F1
Wanstead (LT) 40A2
Wanstead Park (SL) 40B2
Wapping (LT) 40C4
Warblington (SC) 4E2
Ware (WN) 11F3
Wareham (SW) 3F4
Wargrave (TT) 4A1/10G2
Warham Halt (Pres) 18D5
Warminster (WE) 3C4
Warnham (SC) 5D2
Warrington Bank Quay (VT) 15A1/20C2/24G2/45D4
Warrington Central (NW) 15A1/20C2/24G2/45D4
Warwick (CT) 10B5
Warwick Parkway (CH) 11G1
Washford (Pres) 8E5
Watchet (Pres) 8E5
Water Orton (CT) 15F5
Waterbeach (WN) 11C4
Wateringbury (SE) 6C5
Waterloo (AM) 20B4/24F4/45F3
Waterthorpe (SYS) 41A3
Watford (LT) 5A2/11G1
Watford High Street (SL) 5A2/11G1
Watford Junction (SL) 5A2/11G1
Watford North (SL) 11G1
Watford Stadium (SL) 5A2/11G1
Watford West (SL) 5A2/11G1
Watlington (WN) 17E4
Watton at Stone (WN) 11F2
Waunfawr (Pres) 19E2
Waun-Gron Park (CA) 43B4
Wavertree Technology Park (NW) 45F4
Wedgwood (CT) 15D3/20F1
Wednesbury Great Western Street (Midland Metro) 13B2
Wednesbury Parkway (Midland Metro) 13B2
Weeley (GE) 12E3

INDEX OF FREIGHT AND OTHER NON-PASSENGER TERMINALS

Note: A number of these locations are no longer regularly served although the route remains intact but disused. These locations, such as Wirksworth, Wisbech and Portishead, are shown for the sake of completeness. A number of these lines, such as those to Wirksworth, are now the subject of preservation projects. A number of other ex-freight lines, such as the lines to Amlwch and Eastgate, are now to be regarded as preservation schemes and the stations have been transferred to the 'open' stations index.

INDEX OF CLOSED STATIONS

Note: This atlas is not intended to show all closed stations but those that enable closed lines to be placed into context with the surviving lines. For a comprehensive gazetteer of all stations in the British Isles, readers are referred to *Atlas and Gazetteer of Station Names* by Tony Dewick.

Kinnerley Junction	14A1	Mitre Bridge	39C4	Pudsey Greenside	42A4	Sutton Bridge	17E4
Kinross	30A3	Moffat	30G3	Quainton Road	10E3	Swaffham	18F5
Kippax	42B1	Mold	20D5	Queensbury	42B5	Tadcaster	21D4
Kirkburton	21E2	Moniaive	26A5	Ramsey	11B2	Tavistock	1C5
Kirkburton	42D4	Monmouth May Hill	8A2/9E1	Ramsey North	11A2/17G2	Tayport	34E4
Kirkintilloch	29B5/44C5	Monmouth Troy	8A2/9E1	Redwharf Bay & Benllech	19C2	Tenbury Wells	9A1
Kirkudbright	26C5	Morebath	7F5	Reedsmouth	27A3	Tetbury	9F3
Kirriemuir	34C4	Moretonhampstead	2B4	Renfrew Potterfield	44F4	Tewkesbury	9D3
Knott End	24C4	Much Wenlock	15F2	Renfrew South	44F4	Thame	10E3
Lambourn	4A4/10G5	Muirkirk	29E5	Riccarton Junction	31G1	Thaxted	11E4
Lampeter	13E5	Mumbles Pier	7B3	Richmond (Yorks)	27F5	The Dyke	5F3
Langholm	26A1	Muswell Hill	5A3	Ringwood	4E5	Thornbury	8B1/9F2
Lauder	31D1	Mynydd-y-Garreg	7A2	Ripon	21B3	Thrapston	10A1/11B1
Laxfield	12B3	Nailsworth	9F3	Rishworth	21E1	Three Cocks Junction	14F2
Ledston	21D4	Nantlle	19E2	Robin Hood	42B2	Tillynaught	37C2
Leek	15B4	New Radnor	14E2	Rosedale	28F3	Tintern	8B2
Leith	30B2	New Romney &		Roskear	1E4	Tiverton	2A3
Lennoxtown	29B5	Littlestone-on-Sea	6E3	Ross-on-Wye	9D1	Tollesbury	12F5
Leslie	34G5	Newbiggin-by-the-Sea	28A5	Rothbury	31G4	Tolleshunt D'Arcy	12F5
Leuchars Old Station	34E4	Newcastle Emlyn	13F3	Royton	45A2	Torrington	7G3
Leysdown	6B3	Newcastleton	27A1	Ruddington	16D4/41G4	Towcester	10C3
Llanfyllin	14A3	Newent	9D2	Ruthin	20E5	Tresavean	1E5
Llanmorlais	7B3	Newport	4F3	Rye Harbour	6E4	Truro (Newham)	1E1
Loch Tay	33E2	Newport (Salop)	15E2	Ryeland	29D5	Turnchapel	1D5
Lochty	34F4	Newport Pagnell	10C2	Saffron Walden	11D4	Van	14C4
Lofthouse in Nidderdale	21B2	Newton Stewart	25B4	Sandgate	6D2	Ventnor	4G3
(London) Broad Street	5A3	Newtyle	34D5	Sandwich Road	6C2	Ventnor Town	4G3
Long Melford	12D5	Neyland	7D2	Scholes	42A2	Vobster	3B3/8E1
Longridge	24D2	North Leith	30B2	Scotsgap	27A4	Wadebridge	1C2
Lossiemouth	36B2	Norwich City	18F3	Seahouses	31E5	Wantage	10F5
Louth	17A3/22G2	Oakamoor	15C4	Sedbergh	24A2/27G2	Warboys	11B2
Lunton	7E4	Old Meldrum	37E3	Selkirk	30E1	Waskerley	27D4
Lybster	38E2	Oldbury	13B2/15G4	Selsey	4F1	Waterhouses	15C4
Lydbrook Junction	8A2/9E1	Oundle	11A1/17G1	Shepton Mallet	3C3/8E1	Wath-on-Dearne	42E1
Lyme Regis	3F1	Padstow	1C2	Shipston-on-Stour	9C5	Watlington	10F3
Mablethorpe	17B2	Palace Gates	5A3/40A5	Sidmouth	2B2	Wearhead	27D3
Macduff	37C2	Pateley Bridge	21B2	Silloth	26C3	Wells	3C2
Machrihanish	29F1	Peebles	30D2	Snailbeach	14B1	Wenford	1C3
Macmerry	30B1	Peel	23B2	Southwell	16C3	West Bay	3F1
Maldon East & Heybridge	12F5	Penicuik	30C2	Southwold	12B1	West Moors	3E5
Malmesbury	9F3	Penybontfawr	14A3	Spilsby	17B3	Westerham	5C4
Market Drayton	15D2/20F2	Perranporth	1D1	St Andrews	34F4	Wetherby	21C4
Market Weighton	22D5	Peterhead	37D5	St Boswells	31E1	Whithorn	25D4
Marlborough	4A5	Piel	24B5	St Combs	37C5	Whitton	22E4
Maryfield	34E4	Plymstock	1D5	St John's	23B2	Willow Walk	40D4
Masham	21A3	Ponteland	27B5	Staines West	5B2	Wimborne	3E5
Maud Junction	37D4	Port Carlisle	26C2	Stainland &		Wingham	6C2
Melmerby	21A3	Port Victoria	6B4	Holywell Green	21E2/42C5	Withernsea	22E2
Meltham	21F2/42D5	Porthcawl	7C5/43E4	Stanley	42B2	Woodhead	21F2/42F5
Melton Constable	18D4	Portland	3G3	Steyning	5F2	Wooperton	31E4
Middleton	20B1/24F1/45A2	Portpatrick	25C1	Stoke Ferry	11A5/17F5	Yarmouth	4F4
Middleton-in-Teesdale	27E3	Portreath	1E5	Stourport	9A3	Yeadon	21D2
Midhurst	4D1	Potterhill	44G3	Strathaven Central	29D5	Yealmpton	2E5
Mildenhall	11B5	Presteign	14D2	Strathaven North	29D5		
Minsterley	14B1	Princetown	2C5	Strathpeffer	35D5		